FORGIVE-
NESS IS
A WORK
AS WELL AS A
GRACE

FORGIVE-NESS IS A WORK AS WELL AS A GRACE

Edna Hong

AUGSBURG Publishing House • Minneapolis

Scripture quotations unless otherwise noted are from the Revised Standard Version of the Bible, copyright 1946, 1952, and 1971 by the Division of Christian Education of the National Council of Churches.

Scripture quotations marked JB are from The Jerusalem Bible, copyright © 1966 by Doubleday & Company, Inc.

Library of Congress Cataloging in Publication Data

Hong, Edna Hatlestad, 1913-
    FORGIVENESS IS A WORK AS WELL AS A GRACE.

    1. Forgiveness.   2. Forgiveness of sin.   3. Prayers.
I. Title.
BJ1476.H66   1984   234'.5   84-6470
ISBN 0-8066-2081-1

Manufactured in the U.S.A.   APH 10-2356

1   2   3   4   5   6   7   8   9   0   1   2   3   4   5   6   7   8   9

*This book is dedicated
with love and gratitude
to
Mary and Carroll Hinderlie*

We hear of many who are eating their heart out
because circumstances do not allow them a fuller life.
But it is not more life and fuller that we want.
We need a different life,
a life not simply with a new light in it
but a new power in it and a new footing under it.
We need a new center,
not a transformation but a transposition.
We need the completion
not of the soul but of its radical change.
A new order of life and love
A new ethic born of the spirit.

P. T. Forsythe

Contents

Acknowledgments

Unless otherwise noted, quotations from Søren Kierkegaard are from *Søren Kierkegaard's Journals and Papers,* vol. 2, © 1970 by Indiana University Press. Used by permission.

The quotation from Martin Luther on pp. 24-25 is from *Day by Day We Magnify Thee,* © by Epworth Press, London. Used by Permission.

The quotations from Martin Luther on pp. 44 and 77 are from *What Luther Says,* © 1959 Concordia Publishing House. Used by permission.

Quotations from Hanns Lilje are from *The Valley of the Shadow,* © 1950 by Fortress Press. Used by permission.

The quotation from P. T. Forsythe on p. 4 is from *The Creative Theology of P. T. Forsythe,* ed. by Samuel J. Mikolaski, published by William B. Eerdmans Publishing Co. Used by permission.

The quotations from P. T. Forsythe on pp. 46-47, 76, and 97 are from *The Cure of Souls,* ed. by Harry Escott, published by William B. Eerdmans Publishing Co. and George Allen & Unwin (Publishers) Ltd. Used by permission.

The quotations from Laurens van der Post on pp. 70-75 are from *The Seed and the Sower,* © 1963 by Laurens van der Post. Used by permission of William Morrow and Company and The Hogarth Press.

Quotations from the Brothers Karamazov by Fyodor Dostoevski are from the Random House edition of the translation by Constance Garnett.

Quotations from *Crime and Punishment* by Fyodor Dostoevski are from the Fine Editions Press edition of the translation by Constance Garnett.

Preface

Four years ago I wrote *The Downward Ascent,* sent it off to the publisher, and packed away my writing gear. At the time I felt that in this slim little book I had said what I wanted to say, said it plainly, and I was done with it. But the book was not done with me, and I should have ended it with a semicolon and not a period (actually, I ended it with an exclamation point). For some time now the book has clamored to be rounded out and completed, has called for a sequel.

When an author is visited by a notion to write a sequel to something, she or he should refuse to be an easy mark—indeed, should close the door in its face firmly and shoot the lock loudly.

May I go on record as saying that I did precisely that, but the notion scurried around to the back door and had its foot in before I could lock it.

"Go away!" I said. "I'm not admitting your idea. Every sequel I know has been a disaster. Moreover, sequels taste like a warmed-over tuna-fish-potato-chip hotdish. No, thanks!"

I squeezed the back door on its foot, but without flinching, the sequel-notion looked me square in the eye. "You know very well that *The Downward Ascent* was strong on the descent but weak on the ascent. It did not ascend to the last point of vision and descend to earth again with the glad swoop of assurance of the forgiveness of sins."

"And what else was wrong?" I asked thornily.

"You did not describe the state of forgiveness, life in the state of forgiveness."

So, here it is, a sequel to *The Downward Ascent,* which should have ended with a semicolon, even if semicolons are out of fashion.

1

A Brand-new State!

And for anyone who is in Christ, there is a new creation;
the old creation has gone, and now the new one is here.
It is all God's work. It was God who reconciled us to himself
through Christ and gave us the work of handing on this
reconciliation.

2 Corinthians 5:17-19 JB

There is not one moral virtue that Jesus inculcated but
Plato and Cicero did inculcate before him. What then did
Jesus inculcate? Forgiveness of sins. This alone is the
Gospel, and this is the Life and Immortality brought to light
in Jesus.

William Blake

Prayer Meditation

Our Father in heaven, you gave each of your earth children
the human power to forgive. We thank you that we are
humanly able to forgive each other our mean and hateful

acts. But we cannot forgive ourselves, Lord! We cannot forgive our own meanness and hatefulness. We cannot heal the cancer at the marrowbone of our beings.

But even that you have taken care of, Father of us all. In your love for us you have freely forgiven us in your Son Jesus Christ, a miracle so amazing that we have not grasped the wonder of it, a condition so brand-new in human history that we do not know how to receive it or to use it.

Oh, teach us, dear Father! Teach us that you are not only a God of forgiveness but that you in very fact and act can accomplish it in us. We pray not for a Sunday sense of forgiveness. We pray not for momentary acts of forgiveness. We pray for the spirit of forgiveness. We pray for the power of will to emigrate from our present state and to move into the new state your Son Jesus Christ created for us, the state of forgiveness. We pray that we may become fully naturalized citizens of the state of forgiveness. We pray in your Son's name. Amen.

A friend well past his three score years and ten lay dying in a nursing home, but death was irksomely slow about coming.

One morning a very young and newly hired aide came in with his breakfast tray. "Good morning, Al! How are you this morning?"

"Well," answered our friend, a twinkle in his faded blue eyes, "one of these mornings you are going to come in and find me in the state of rigor mortis."

The bright smile faded and became slightly embarrassed and apologetic.

"I haven't traveled as much as other kids my age," she said. "I've never been in that state."

When it comes to our spiritual lives, it is the state of spiritual rigor mortis that we human beings make our habitation. Indeed, we seem to find it quite habitable and are quite habituated to it. The state of forgiveness is the state in which we have never been. We are quite content to catch a glimpse of it every time we forgive another or are forgiven in single acts of forgiveness. But move into that state, make it our home state, become naturalized citizens and live by the laws of that state, speak the language of that state? No, thank you!

Yet here it is—close enough to grasp! Here—not over and across and beyond a Himalayan mountain range. Now— not in some by-and-by or some blissful millenium. A brand-new state! Brand-new in human history! Founded by Jesus Christ for sinners who wish to be rescued from themselves. A state for victims who wish to be rescued from the consequences of their own acts. A state where forgiven sinners forgive as they are forgiven. A state where it is second nature to forgive as one is forgiven. A state whose citizens create a redemptive community.

Impossible? Politically, yes. After all, politics is only the art of the possible. As citizens of a political state we remain nibblers of the possible. But Christ has called us to seize the impossible, to be graspers of the impossible. Even to forgiving our enemies!

Forgive our enemies! That really sounds beautiful when we hear the preacher talk about it in the pulpit. It's a beautiful thought to take home and carry around in our minds—until there is an enemy we have to forgive from the heart, a real-life enemy. Then it becomes impossible.

In one of her TV comedy series in which she plays homely, cross-grained Eunice, Carol Burnett portrays Eunice returning with her equally ill-favored husband from a revival meeting where they have heard an inspiring sermon on forgiveness. Eunice dashes to the phone to call her sister, who is everything Eunice is not—pretty, popular, and prosperously married. With good reason Eunice has hated her shallow, selfish sister since childhood, but now, on the beautiful wings of the beautiful thought of forgiveness, she flies to the phone. Of course, I cannot remember the lines and can only approximate my memory of the powerful and sad—certainly not funny—impact of the playlet.

"Sister, dear! We just heard the most *marvelous* sermon on forgiveness. It was simply *beautiful!* I could hardly wait to come home and call you up and forgive you. Yes, sister dear, I am forgiving you everything! *Everything!* Absolutely every mean, dirty thing you said and did to me all my life. Even the time you stole my date for the junior-senior prom. Remember? You had about a dozen invites, and I didn't have a single one. But when you heard that Don Matson was thinking of asking me, you took him. You got a brand-new formal and went off to the prom looking like a princess, and I sat home. . . . Yes, you did, sister, dear! You did, too. . . . You did, you did, *you did!!* And you've done things to me all my life! Even last week you didn't invite me to lunch when Judy Pickens was back in town. She was my friend *first.* Remember? But you stole her away from me, too. . . . Yes, you did, too! You did, you did, *you did!!* All you've ever done is take, take, take. . . . Don't tell me to shut up! . . . Who's screaming? . . . Why did I call you anyway? I called you to forgive you. Do you hear? *Forgive!* But you spoiled even that. All your life you've spoiled things for me, and now you've even spoiled my wanting to forgive you!"

Who can laugh at Eunice? Who can condemn her? Certainly not we who, although believing and confessing the doctrine of the forgiveness of sins, do not happily, speedily, and confidently move into that state of grace but continue to live in the spiritual state of morbidity and rigor mortis, speaking its bleak language of complaints, accusations, and laments. Certainly not we who form a procession to the altar to receive "the gracious forgiveness of all your sins," feed on Christ's body and drink his blood, and then go home and continue to feed on our secret despair, disappointments, fears, frustrations, griefs, grudges, and hatreds. If the prodigal son had sat moping through the banquet his father prepared for him, it would have been no more incongruous.

In short, the state of forgiveness, sad to say, seems to be rather sparsely populated. Many of us have to confess with considerable embarrassment that we have never been in that state. Not to have moved into the state of forgiveness must mean that there is something rotten in the state of you and the state of me. Is failure to move out of my preceding state of sin into the state of forgiveness *a new sin?*

2

Then Why Do We Not Move In?

Let it be known to you therefore, brethren, that through this man forgiveness of sins is proclaimed to you, and by him every one that believes is freed from everything from which you could not be freed by the law of Moses. Beware, therefore, lest there come upon you what is said in the prophets: "Behold, you scoffers, and wonder, and perish; for I do a deed in your days, a deed you will never believe, if one declares it to you."   Acts 13:38-41

The forgiveness of sins is proclaimed, but who marvels at it? No one. No one says: Is it possible—oh, is it possible? No one believes it and says: It is possible, it is possible! No one wonders; no one is scandalized.

Søren Kierkegaard

Prayer Meditation

Our Father, we are born-and-brought-up Christians. All our lives we have heard your love for us and your forgiveness through the death of your Son on the cross proclaimed to us. And yet, Father, we go on living by the natural laws

21

of reaction and retaliation. We smash relationships right and left. We live among smashed relationships: between wives and husbands, between parents and children, between mothers-in-law and daughters-in-law, between neighbors, between employers and employees, between teachers and pupils, between pastors and congregations, between business partners, business rivals, between peoples, between nations. Everywhere, everywhere—hurts that need forgiving, wounds that need healing!

Father, forgive us for ignoring the new way of forgiveness your Son made for us that leads into the state of forgiveness. Forgive us for not making it a beaten path.

Father, this time we do not pray, "Lord, have mercy on us." Instead we pray that you not be gentle with us. Please send us your Holy Prodder and have him push, shove, and pummel us onto Christ's new way, Christ's highway of living and loving and forgiving. In his name. Amen.

Then why do we not move? If we really believe in the forgiveness of our sins, why do we not up and move into the state of forgiveness and live there instead of stubbornly remaining in our former state? Are we afraid to leave our dear familiar ruts and live in the latitude of forgiveness, afraid that we will toss and roll around in all that gracious space? After all, did not God place me in my own personal rut?

Perhaps the climate over there in the new state is harsh and unhealthful. Nonsense! Could there be a harsh climate in a state where everything that is harsh, hateful, and sinful in relationships is supposed to fall away? Where the clenched fist is supposed to unclench in the sun of forgiveness? Indeed, must not the climate there be like the air at twilight when the earth forgives the sun for the heat of the day? Or when the wind brings rain and the parched ground forgives the wind for holding back the rain so long?

Are we perhaps afraid of the citizenry of the state of forgiveness? Afraid that in their forgiven state they will be God cuddlers and Jesus freaks and have a cloying birthday-cake look? Nice people can be very disagreeable neighbors. Would we rather live as neighbors to neurotics?

Are we afraid that in the state of forgiveness we will bask in bliss and forget the underside of the world? That we will drop out of the world, forget its need for reconciliation, and be concerned only for our own personal salvation, for our own good and goods? That our blissful unemployed or underemployed hearts will dance in eternal celebration of our own salvation? If so, we would rather reel and stagger with the have-nots to the cacophonies of the world than dance with the haves to their heavenly harmonies.

Perhaps we want to be absolutely certain of our forgiveness before we move into the state of forgiveness. We do not want to be tricked into a utopian dream and be skinned, as our kin are sometimes taken in by supersalespersons selling glamorous and "fully developed" lots in the sunshine states. Two of our kin purchased such lots. One turned out to be in the Mohave Desert, 10 miles from the farthest edge of the nearest town. The other is several miles distant from the promised water access to the Gulf of Mexico. The lots, of course, were purchased sight unseen. (Why does that remind me of a Japanese translation of "out of sight, out of mind"—"invisible, insane"?)

Being sensible, intelligent, prudent Christians, we are wary of a state not to be found in any atlas, and we cannot believe what we cannot see. Lacking exact and reliable information about the authenticity and workability of a state of forgiveness, we elect to stay where we are. Moreover, if we did elect to move, we could not stand the tension between certainty about forgiveness and the uncertainty that, in our opinion, would be inevitable. After all, we may be forgiven, but we are not instant saints!

Then, too, even if we could overcome our doubts about being forgiven, could we ever cease doubting our own ability to forgive? (How humble that sounds! It has the ring of a truly deep nature!) After all, is not the law of vengeance printed indelibly onto our fallen human nature? Indeed, it has prevailed in every culture under the sun since the fall, and has even reigned as a code of honor. The "noble" Greeks either killed their captives or made them slaves. Moreover, Greece was noted not only for its physical and mental athletes, but also for its litigious citizens, who went to court at the drop of a real or imagined slur. Paul scolded the Christians in Corinth for their lawsuits against each other and told them that they ought to be ashamed of themselves (1 Cor. 6:1-11). Various tribes of American Indians had hereditary enemies, and in some cases they had no memory of when, why, or where the enmity started. The law of "a life for a life" ruled on the frontier and in remote mountain valleys in the United States until quite recently. *Khul-Khaal,* a recently published book in which five Egyptian women tell their stories, tells of hatreds and grudges—both ancient

24

and new—so virulent that weddings and funerals, which bring families and friends and acquaintances together for an extended time, often turn into violence and bloodshed. "Egypt is 10% love and 90% hate," said one of these women, and she spoke not of the government but of what governs human hearts.

Can anyone honestly say that class and race hatreds have been wiped out in the United States? Perhaps among Christians? Some of the most virulent hatreds I have ever heard of exist today in Christian congregations! A reliable source told me of a church council member, a woman, who hates the pastor so much that she comes to church every Sunday, sits up front, and reads the Sunday paper throughout the sermon. A preacher's widow, herself the victim, reported being denied entrance at a church women's meeting in a private home and being told, "You are not welcome here."

Yes, sad to say, the law of vengeance still lingers in our midst. Yet we seem to prefer it (because it is so familiar?) and are skeptical of this new state with new and unfamiliar laws.

Aha! There's the rub, the real stickler! We are afraid of the *laws* in the state of forgiveness. Sure, it is preached to be a state of grace, but somehow law always seems to sneak into what is proclaimed as pure grace. What about "Forgive as you have been forgiven"? Is not that a "Thou shalt"? Indeed, the Lord's Prayer petitions, "Forgive us our sins as we forgive those who sin against us." If this is not laying down a condition, then what is a condition? And grace is supposed to have no conditions! We can be pretty sure that the police cars of the conscience will be cruising around in the state of forgiveness to see if we have met the conditions and kept the laws.

No, thank you! The state of forgiveness may be all right for God and company—and saints—but not for us bottom-rungers who make no claim to be saints. Forgiven sinners we may be, but we remain flesh, bone, and tissue. We still have our all-too-human psyches. If we are burned, we jerk away. If our pride is burned, we jerk away. If we break a bone, we hurt. If a relationship is broken, we hurt. We avoid skunks. We avoid people who are a stench in the nostrils of our psyches. (An old proverb: Fresh fish and guests both stink after three days.) We shun poison ivy. We shun people who irritate us. We hate fire and steam and all that gives us pain. We hate people who deliberately and maliciously give us pain, people who would never let themselves be guilty of murdering us, but whose faces plainly say, "I wish you were dead!"

The state of forgiveness? Live in the state of forgiveness? There are persons in our lives we cannot imagine ourselves forgiving until they are in a state of rigor mortis. Therefore the state of forgiveness is not for us!

3

We Are Not Alone
in Malingering

And behold, they brought to him a paralytic, lying on his
bed; and when Jesus saw their faith he said to the paralytic, "Take heart, my son; your sins are forgiven." And
behold, some of the scribes said to themselves, "This man
is blaspheming." But Jesus, knowing their thoughts, said,
"Why do you think evil in your hearts? For which is easier,
to say, 'Your sins are forgiven,' or to say, 'Rise and walk'?
But that you may know that the Son of man has authority
on earth to forgive sins"—he then said to the paralytic—
"Rise, take up your bed and go home." And he rose and
went home.

Matthew 9:2-8

It is the road—which is the shadow cast by the Cross upon
all "healthy" human life, which is the place where the
tenacity of men is invisibly, yet most effectually, disturbed
and shattered and dissolved; the place where the com-
petence of God, of the Spirit, of Eternity, can enter within
our horizon.

Karl Barth

And as I entered my twenties, the spiritual sensitiveness began to strengthen. I found myself isolated from the Churches not so much by my paganism as by my awareness of movements on the eternal frontier. I was watchful and expectant and sometimes afraid. I could not reach beyond the frontier, but something from beyond it was reaching me, leading me to recognition of the basic fallacy of the unregenerate search for God. In moments of tranquillity I caught the first gleams of the truth that finally solved my problem, the fact that the ultimate step towards Christianity is not a search but a surrender.

Jack Clemo, *The Invading Gospel*

Prayer Meditation

Father, I'm sick of being stingy with forgiveness! I'm bored to death with my dingy life on the border of your kingdom, the state of forgiveness. I'm tired of being a pious procrastinator. I'm sick to death of being a spiritual paralytic.

Holy Spirit of forgiveness, make me drop all my petty hates and grudges at the border and *leap.* In one hand I will clutch my permanent visa for the state of forgiveness, your gift to me in Christ, for which I thank and praise you, Father! Take my other hand, Holy Spirit, and lead me dancing, whistling, and singing into the state of forgiveness! Amen.

In the Chartres Cathedral there is a sculpture that may not rank with Michelangelo's Sistine Chapel painting of God creating Adam, but certainly is not outclassed by it in the depth and feeling of its conception. It shows naked man kneeling beside Christ, his head resting in perfect peace and joy in Christ's lap and under his tenderly touching hands. The sculpture is entitled "God Creating Adam"—that is, the new Adam that is created by the uncreating of his sins by Jesus Christ!

Yet many a person, many a Christian person, stops at the border of the state of forgiveness and does not move into the joyful fullness of relationship to God through his Son's work in uncreating our sins. We linger—and wait for death to "cure" our malingering and malignancies.

We do not walk alone in our difficulty to believe in and live in the state of forgiveness of our sins. Indeed, we are a multitude, a heterogeneous crowd, numbering some rather impressive spiritual leaders and thinkers.

Luther's tortured search for a gracious and forgiving God is familiar to us. He never doubted that Christ was the Son of God, but it was a long time before he could believe in the forgiveness of his sins in and through Christ. His breakthrough to that truth changed his life and changed theology. But let us never forget that days and nights of spiritual struggle preceded the bold confidence that enabled him to preach on the text "Take heart, my son; your sins are forgiven" and say:

> It is easily said, forgiveness of sins. Ah, if it could be won and done with words! But when it comes to the serious encounter, nothing is known of it. For it is a great thing, which I must believe and grasp with my heart, namely, that all my sins are forgiven and that through this faith I am justified before God. That is a wonderful justice and very different from the justice of the judges and of the wise

and prudent people in the world. For they all say that justice is to be found within man's heart and soul as a quality wrought into it. But this Gospel teaches us that Christian righteousness is not a quality within man's heart or soul; but we should learn that we are redeemed and made just through the forgiveness of sins.

Søren Kierkegaard, too, had a painful and difficult time moving from a steadfast belief in Christ as the Son and revelation of God to a belief in the forgiveness of his sins in Christ. A born-and-brought-up Christian, he nevertheless was subject to moods of deep depression, which he tried to submerge in enormous mental activity.

At the age of 34 Kierkegaard wrote in his journal: "God's eye has spotted me in my conscience, and now it has been made impossible for me to forget that this eye sees me. Having been looked at by God, I had to and have to look to God."

Later that year, having finished and delivered to the publisher the manuscript for *Works of Love,* he wrote:

Something is stirring within me which hints at a metamorphosis. That is why I dare not go to Berlin, for that would induce abortion; therefore I will be quiet, by no means work too hard, not even hard, and will not begin a new book, but try to find myself and, *here where I am,* to think through the idea of my melancholy with God. In this way my melancholy may be lifted and *Christianity may come closer to me.* Up to now I have armed against my depression with intellectual activity which keeps it away— now, in the faith that God has forgotten in forgiveness whatever guilt I have, I must try to forget it myself, but not in any diversion, not in any distance from it, but in God,

so that when I think of God I may think that he has forgotten it and in that way myself learn to dare to forget it
in forgiveness.

Søren Kierkegaard's breakthrough came at Easter time in
1848. "Maundy Thursday and Good Friday have become
truly holy days for me." Yet his healing was not complete,
and on Easter Monday he wrote, "I do believe in the forgiveness of sins, but I interpret this, as before, to mean that
I must bear my punishment of remaining in this painful
prison of inclosing reserve all my life, in a more profound
sense separated from the company of other men, yet miti-
gated by the thought that God has forgiven me."

In July of 1848 Kierkegaard jotted down his plan to write
a new book, the title to be:

The Radical Cure
or
The Forgiveness of Sin and Atonement

Unfortunately for the world, Kierkegaard never wrote the
book, but the books he did write diagnose humankind's
"sickness unto death," despair, with the penetration of one
who had himself acutely suffered from the same sickness.
As was his custom, he described all aspects and levels of
the sickness, labeling the most intense form the break with
faith in Christ and the forgiveness of sins. But at all times
he balanced his diagnosis, which left no hidden cancer of
the psyche or soul undetected, with the healing and the
cure. Whether he was describing the sickness or the cure,
his descriptions have the surprise of originality. For example,
"It is the Deity's joy to forgive sins; just as God is almighty
in creating out of nothing, so he is almighty in uncreating

31

something, for to forget, almightily to forget, is indeed to uncreate something." Amazing thought! Our God is Creator and Uncreator!

C. S. Lewis's reluctance to enter the Kingdom (the state of forgiveness!) is described in his book *Surprised by Joy*. All pious prodigals who are malingering should read it.

In literature, it is Ivan Karamazov in Dostoevski's *The Brothers Karamazov* who is the tragic example of the intellectually honest individual who stands at the frontier of the kingdom and passionately wishes to cross over but in the end gives back his entrance ticket. Ivan could not reconcile innocent suffering and the beastliness of all-too-human beings with the conception of a wise, just, and loving God. In a long and passionate dialog with his brother Alyosha he says:

> "Listen! I took the case of children only to make my case clearer. Of the other tears of humanity with which the earth is soaked from its crust to its centre, I will say nothing. I have narrowed my subject on purpose. I am a bug, and I recognize in all humility that I cannot understand why the world is arranged as it is. Men are themselves to blame, I suppose; they were given paradise, they wanted freedom, and stole fire from heaven, though they knew they would become unhappy, so there is no need to pity them. . . . For the hundredth time I repeat, there are numbers of questions, but I've only taken the children, because in their case what I mean is so unanswerably clear. Listen! If all must suffer to pay for the eternal harmony, what have children to do with it, tell me, please? It's beyond all comprehension why they should suffer, and why they should pay for the harmony. . . . What do I care for a hell for

oppressors? What good can hell do, since those children have already been tortured? And what becomes of harmony, if there is hell? I want to forgive. I want to embrace. I don't want more suffering. And if the sufferings of children go to swell the sum of sufferings which was necessary to pay for truth, then I protest that the truth is not worth such a price. . . . Is there in the whole world a being who would have the right to forgive and could forgive? I don't want harmony. From love for humanity I don't want it. I would rather be left with the unavenged suffering. I would rather remain with my unavenged suffering and unsatisfied indignation *even if I were wrong*. . . . And so I hasten to give back my entrance ticket, and if I am an honest man I am bound to give it back as soon as possible. And that I am doing. It's not God that I don't accept, Alyosha, only I must respectfully return Him the ticket."

"That's rebellion," murmured Alyosha, looking down.

"Rebellion? I am sorry you call it that," said Ivan earnestly. "One can hardly live in rebellion, and I want to live. Tell me yourself, I challenge you—answer. Imagine that you are creating a fabric of human destiny with the object of making men happy in the end, giving them peace and rest at last, but that it was essential and inevitable to torture to death only one tiny creature—that baby beating its breast with its fist, for instance—and to found that edifice on its unavenged tears, would you consent to be the architect on those conditions? Tell me, and tell the truth."

"No, I wouldn't consent," said Alyosha softly.

"And can you admit the idea that men for whom you are building it would agree to accept their happiness on the foundation of the unexpiated blood of a little victim? And accepting it would remain happy for ever?"

"No, I can't admit it, Brother," said Alyosha suddenly, with flashing eyes, "you said just now, is there a being in the whole world who would have the right to forgive and could forgive? But there is a Being and He can forgive everything, all and for all, because He gave His innocent blood for all and everything. You have forgotten Him, and on Him is built the edifice, and it is to Him they cry aloud, 'Thou art just, O Lord, for Thy ways are revealed!' ''

4

Forgiveness Is for Life, Not Death

As therefore you received Christ Jesus the Lord, so live in him.

Colossians 2:6

Put to death therefore what is earthly in you. . . .put them all away: anger, wrath, malice, slander, and foul talk from your mouth. Do not lie to one another, seeing that you have put off the old nature with its practices and have put on the new nature, which is being renewed in knowledge after the image of its creator.

Colossians 3:5-10

With him are strength and wisdom; the deceived and the deceiver are his. He uncovers the deep out of darkness, and brings deep darkness to light.

Job 12:16, 22

Cannot this experience of the most beautiful and precious gifts of God, on the very brink of death, be given to men in the midst of life?

Hanns Lilje, *The Valley of the Shadow*

Prayer Meditation

Our Father, why do old grudges die only when the grudger and the begrudged die? Why do mothers-in-law never in life forgive their daughters-in-law for marrying their sons? Or daughters-in-law never forgive their mothers-in-law for never forgiving them for marrying their sons? Why do we wait until the ornery old grandfather dies before we see him in a forgiving light? Why do we wait to visit the crotchety old aunt in the funeral parlor visitation when we totally ignored her all those years she lived in the retirement home? Why do nations go to war and fight each other to defeat and death (even though victory is a defeat and death) before they reconcile? Why, oh why, Lord?

Our Father, your servant Paul bade us shed the shabby clothes of our old nature and put on the brand-new clothes of our new nature. Spirit of the living, loving God, strip off the rags of our unforgivingness now while we live! Let us discard them at the border, dress up in the clothes of forgiveness, and enter the state of forgiveness. In your Son's name. Amen.

Few there are who write their own epitaphs. Jonathan Swift, who saw and brilliantly satirized our human foibles, did, and it was placed on his tombstone.

Ubi saeva indignatio ulterius cor lacerare nequit
[Where fierce indignation can no longer tear the heart]

Death is indeed a sure cure for the diseases of the flesh, but it cannot heal or rescue that which flesh has housed in this mortal life—the spirit. Yet death does seem to have a temporary mitigating effect on the grudging spirits and bitter feelings and stony hearts of those who stand in the presence of the dying or the dead. Death seems to be able to do what could not be done in the dead or dying during one's lifetime—improve his or her public esteem and extinguish the negatives in his or her character. We are even willing to forgive our enemies, rivals, critics, and detractors—when they are dead. Families that have been irreconcilable for years will forgive their most disagreeable member—when he or she is dead.

In his play *A Woman of No Importance,* Oscar Wilde has a character say, "Children begin by loving their parents, after a time they judge them, rarely if ever do they forgive them." As a rule children *do* forgive their parents—when they are dead. "All that was earthly, harsh, and sinful in our relation has fallen away; all that was holy in it remains," wrote Thomas Carlyle of his dead father.

In *The Lifted Veil,* George Eliot had Latimer, the narrator, reflect on this strange propensity to wait until death to forgive.

> I have never fully unbosomed myself to any human being; I have never been encouraged to trust much in the sympathy of my fellow-men. But we have all a chance of meeting with some pity, some tenderness, some charity when we are dead; it is the living only who cannot be forgiven—the living only from whom men's indulgence and reverence are held off, like the rain by the hard east wind. While the heart beats, bruise it—it is your only opportunity; while the eye can still turn toward you with moist, timid entreaty, freeze it with an icy, unanswering gaze; while

the ear, that delicate messenger to the inmost sanctuary of the soul, can still take in the tone of kindness, put it off with hard civility, or sneering compliment, or envious affectation of indifference; while the creative brain can still throb with the sense of injustice, with the yearning for brotherly recognition—make haste—oppress it with your ill-considered judgments, your trivial comparisons, your careless misrepresentations. The heart will by-and-by be still. . .the eye will cease to entreat; the ear will be deaf; the brain will have ceased from all wants as well as from all work. Then your charitable speeches may find vent; then you may remember and pity the toil and the struggle and the failure; then you may give due honor to the work achieved; then you may find extenuation for errors, and may consent to bury them.

Helen Waddell, who took care of her invalid stepmother for 10 years, reflected in a similar vein, but less bitterly and sarcastically, in a letter to her sister.

You know, the one thing I learned out of those last years . . .was that to hate is to be in hell. I didn't actually *hate* Mother, but I had a deep festering grudge against all the ways she had thwarted me, the things she had taken from me—and never a word of thanks; all the sacrifices were on her side.

After she died I suddenly saw my own heart, and I knew that if I had mastered that grudge inwardly as well as outwardly, those years would have been far richer.

I suppose death helps put things under the countenance of eternity. It wasn't that I was sorrier for her after she died—it was partly my pity for her that used to drive me crazy, a mixture of anger and pity comes near to murder.

It was that I had let a grievance poison myself. And a grievance is a kind of cancer of the heart.

Trapped behind the border of the state of forgiveness, lingering and malingering in the state of sin, we forgive the dead but seem to be unable to forgive the living. And we cannot shoot them dead anymore so that we can forgive them in death!

"Do you forgive your enemies?" a priest asked a dying soldier in the Spanish Civil War.

"I have no enemies," answered the dying soldier. "I shot them all."

Dr. Hanns Lilje, bishop of Hannover and secretary of the Lutheran World Federation, was imprisoned by the Nazis during World War II in a purge of Germans suspected of having a part in the unsuccessful plot to assassinate Hitler. Three thousand people were said to have been put to death at this time, and many more were imprisoned, Bishop Lilje among them. In a quiet but poignant book, *The Valley of the Shadow,* Bishop Lilje described Christmas Eve, 1944, in the Gestapo prison in Berlin.

Christmas was near. Christmas Eve in prison is so terrible because a wave of sentimentality passes through the gloomy building. Everyone thinks of his own loved ones, for whom he is longing; everyone suffers because he doesn't know how they will be celebrating the Festival of Divine and Human Love. Recollections of childhood come surging back, almost overwhelming some, especially those who are condemned to death. . . .

At this time we had a Commandant who was human. Although he had risen from the lower ranks to be an S.S. officer, he had remained an honest man, who, although he was harsh, was not brutal, and who often granted us certain facilities, until, on account of his humane attitude, he was removed from his post. Essentially he made more impression on us than his successor, who, in many respects, was also a decent man.

On this particular evening in the year, this Commandant had made various kind and humane actions possible; for instance, among us there was one who was condemned to death and was already chained. The Commandant had his chains removed, and his violin was given back to him. This man was a great artist, and his playing was like magic. Presently the great vaulted Hall resounded with the beautiful strains of his violin.

Meanwhile, Dr. Lilje walked up and down in his cell, gazing at the nativity scene one of his children had brought him, and thinking of Christmases past. He had just reached the point in his recollections of painfully longing for a congregation to whom he could proclaim the Christmas gospel when he suddenly heard his number called outside his door. Too often this meant interrogations, ill treatment, or still worse. Dr. Lilje followed the guard and was taken to the commandant, who ordered the guard to bring Number 212, the violinist who was under sentence of death. The commandant, without speaking a word, brought the two men to the cell of a condemned prisoner whom Dr. Lilje recognized as Count X, whose brother had been one of the first to be executed after the attempt on Hitler's life. The brother had frequently attended his services, and Dr. Lilje had administered Communion to him the Sunday before his arrest.

Quite spontaneously, forgetting where I was, I mentioned this recollection to X, but the Commandant interrupted me harshly, saying: "I have not brought you gentlemen together for personal conversation!" Then he added, turning to the Count, "You asked that a certain clergyman, your own friend, might be allowed to visit you this evening in a pastoral capacity. Unfortunately I have not been able to accede to this request, but here is Dr. Lilje, who will address some words to you." Now I saw what was expected of me. The Count replied: "What I really want, sir, is to make my confession, and then receive Holy Communion." Immediately I said that I was ready to do what was required; and the Commandant seemed to have no objection. So a small silver cup was brought, a little wine, and some bread. . . .

At the Commandant's suggestion the violinist played a Christmas chorale, exquisitely; then, in this cell, and before this congregation, I read the Gospel for Christmas Day: "Now it came to pass in those days there went out a decree. . . ."

Dr. Lilje spoke briefly about receiving God's great promise and clinging to that promise even in the darkness of death into which the world had been plunged. The count knelt down on the hard stone floor while Dr. Lilje prayed the beautiful old prayer of confession from Thomas á Kempis (which the count himself had chosen) and then pronounced absolution.

It was a very quiet celebration of the Sacrament full of deep confidence in God; almost palpably the wings of the Divine Mercy hovered over us, as we knelt at the altar in a prison cell on Christmas Eve. We were prisoners, in the power of the Gestapo—in Berlin. But the peace of God enfolded us: it was *real* and present, "like a Hand laid gently upon us."

Since the Commandant had obviously done all this without permission, and on his own personal responsibility,

41

he would not allow any further conversation. The violinist played a closing chorale; I parted from my fellow-prisoner with a warm handshake, saying: "God bless you, brother X." When we reached the corridor the Commandant shook my hand twice, with an iron grip; he was deeply moved; turning to me, he said: "Thank you! You cannot imagine what you have done for me this evening, in my sad and difficult daily work."

In the epilog to his beautiful little book, *The Valley of the Shadow,* Dr. Lilje spoke of himself in the third person and in one of the closing paragraphs wrote:

After that royal stillness, in which his imprisonment could do him no harm, since week after week he was able to pray, to meditate, to think, and to pray once more, when he was able to commit his spirit into his Lord's hands, like clay to be moulded by the divine Potter; after that time of quietness, which made him inwardly more free than he had ever been, he will often look back, and will continually ask himself: "Cannot this experience of the most beautiful and precious gifts of God, on the very brink of death, be given to him in the midst of life?"

5

The Human Model of the State of Forgiveness

There was a man who had two sons; and the younger of them said to his father, "Father, give me the share of property that falls to me. . . ."

Luke 15:11-12

Love hides the multiplicity of sins by *forgiveness.*
Søren Kierkegaard

Prayer Meditation

Our Father, when we were very little we played the shadow game with our parents. On sunny days we tried to jump on their shadow heads. They dodged and ducked. But sometimes they let us step on their shadow heads. They cried, "Ouch! Stop! Stop! You're hurting me!" And we screamed with delight.

Our Father, we are parents now. Sometimes our children step on our heads. Sometimes we step on their heads. It is no longer a game, and it really hurts. Our Father, fill us

43

parents, fill our children, with your Son's forgiving love. We ask in his name. Amen.

Do I hear someone (a practical person who wants evidence tangible and solid) sputter: "Sentimental religiousness! There is no such state as your state of forgiveness! Where is the frontier? How does one cross over? If there is a crossing point, what does one leave behind and what does one take over? Is there a rubbish dump at the frontier for the worm bags and sad sacks of our sinful selves? Do we trade in our old natures for new ones? Do we leave behind all our grudges, hatreds, enmities, animosities, alienations, estrangements? Do we strip off our old rags and receive a brand-new wardrobe of stainless, Scotchguarded attitudes, guaranteed not to fade? Humbug! Your state of forgiveness is a pious fraud, and you should be brought to court for swindling the public. This quackery is far worse than duping guileless retirees into buying nonexistent lots in the sunshine states."

Do I hear someone else (a scholar and theologian who steers clear of figurative language) calmly caution: "You are, of course, speaking metaphorically. I suspect that Luther would call you a 'spiritual juggler'. Luther clearly warned against farfetched allegorical and metaphorical interpretations of doctrine. When speaking of faith and doctrine, we are to rely solely on the *nuda Scriptura,* the bare Scripture."

To that I would answer, "Ah, but Luther was a master of beautiful and meaningful metaphors. His hymns are full of them. Of course, he could never come up to his Lord and

44

Master when it came to making metaphors. What was the washing of the disciples' feet but an extended metaphor?"

To which my theologian critic might say, "True! True! And perhaps that is why Luther admonished us to let the Bible make the allegories and, foregoing figurative interpretations, stick to the plain and direct sense of a text or doctrine."

Complying with my critics' fears that I may misuse allegory in interpreting the doctrine of the forgiveness of sins and their insistence that I let *nuda Scriptura* make the allegories, may I introduce the model citizen, the human model of the state of forgiveness. He is the product of Christ's own creative imagination, constructed to teach us what God is like and what forgiveness is all about, to depict for us life literally lived in the state of forgiveness. May I introduce a person who lived by a law as fundamental to the human spirit as the law of gravity to the human body—namely, the law of forgiveness.

Someone has said that the human act of walking is a continual falling. With one foot planted firmly, one thrusts the other foot forward and brings it down to prevent falling, which is the normal response to the law of gravity. Similarly, consciousness of sin and forgiveness of sin evoke each other and are the two dialectical movements, the downward/upward movements, that create a break between the past and the present. Our problem, says Kierkegaard, is "to get the day today unqualified and unprejudiced." Literally believing and exercising the law of forgiveness does just that—makes the day today, the very present now, new in Christ. Personally to receive the condition of forgiveness from God through Christ creates the condition in which forgiveness takes place here and now freely, naturally, and spontaneous-ly—as we see in the model citizen of the state of forgiveness.

The human model of the state of forgiveness has no name. Jesus called this person simply "a man." "A man had two sons." One of them is the lost son, the prodigal son. Hence the man is the father of the prodigal son. Yet by virtue of the condition of forgiveness in which the father lives, he is the only one in the parable who does not regard himself as the father of a prodigal son. His friends and neighbors very likely shook their heads over him, pitied him, and wondered how much more he was going to put up with from this son. What they failed to see was that this father had no limits to what he would put up with. He had crossed the frontier and entered the state of unqualified forgiving love.

This father did not keep an account book of his son's particular sins. He did not forgive for this but not for that, for this something but not for that something. He lived in the state of forgiving love, where forgiveness manifests itself as a law of the spirit and takes place naturally. The father *was* forgiving love.

The son stayed out all night and came home drunk. The father was forgiving love.

The son demanded his share of the estate, wanted his inheritance *now*. He could not wait until the old man was dead. The father divided the estate with him. The father was forgiving love.

The son left his father's house. He spent the money, every penny of it, on a life of debauchery. He wined and dined and womanized. When he had spent his last cent, his friends left him and the women spurned him—even the prostitutes.

He hired out to a pig farmer but did not even receive room and board.

Back at home the father looked down the road and waited—in forgiving love. He was forgiving love even when the son was not there to receive it, even if he were there and spurned it.

The son came to his senses and decided to go back to his father's house. He was willing to be his paid servant, for he did not deserve the relationship of son. While he was still a long way from home, his father saw him, ran to meet him, hugged and kissed him tenderly—for the father was forgiving love.

It was hunger pangs, prudence, and pragmatism—and not true repentance—that brought the prodigal son home to his father's house. Going home was, of course, the only sensible thing to do. But we can be sure that in the clasp of his father's embrace he instantly saw everything in a different light. In the light of that unqualified and unconditional forgiving love that had crossed all the frontiers of worldly wisdom and good common sense, even horse sense, the prodigal son suddenly saw the darkness and depth of his sin.

In that moment two dialectical movements took place in his spirit, creating a clean break with his past. At one and the same time he saw the boundlessness of his father's forgiving love and the enormity of his own sin. Then he truly repented, repented in truth, and if he received his father's forgiveness *literally,* he literally could and would live in "an unqualified and unprejudiced present." He literally could put his past behind his back and celebrate the very present. He could eat the fatted calf as his father's son—not, please note, as the lost son, or even as the lost-and-found son, for in the father's forgiving love he was never lost. The father was in very truth the only one in the parable who did not think of himself as the father of a prodigal son.

"Aha!" my two critics may exclaim at this point. "You are transgressing the limits of both sentimentality and scriptural metaphor. Indeed, you are going beyond Christ! After all, in the prodigal's father Christ is portraying God, and we are not God. You had better look for another model for the human model of the state of forgiveness. If you intend to apply the character of the father in that parable to us human beings, you are arbitrarily and fantastically misusing the parable. You obviously are one of those inexperienced souls Luther said "cannot hold to a sure meaning of Scripture."

6

The Sure Meaning of Scripture

He destined us in love to be his sons through Jesus Christ, according to the purpose of his will, to the praise of his glorious grace which he freely bestowed on us in the Beloved. In him we have redemption through his blood, the forgiveness of our trespasses, according to the riches of his grace which he lavished upon us. For he has made known to us in all wisdom and insight the mystery of his will, according to his purpose which he set forth in Christ as a plan for the fulness of time, to unite all things to him, things in heaven and things on earth.

Ephesians 1:5-10

For repentance, remorse, and knowledge of sin, though necessary, is not enough; faith in the forgiveness of sins in the name of Christ must be added. But where there is such a faith, God no longer sees any sins; for then you stand before God, not in your name but in Christ's name.

Martin Luther

Prayer Meditation

Our Father, most of us are born-and-brought-up Christians. We have gone through the whole Sunday school curriculum. We have read and heard your Word ever since we could lisp the prayer your Son taught us. But, but! But why recite the "buts" to you! You know our "buts" better than we do! We ask only that you forgive them.

Our Father, we do not need a big dictionary and a dozen commentaries to understand your Word. Nor do you ask us to be interpreters. You desire only belief and obedience.

Our Father, your Son came to throw fire on the earth. He said it himself. Send us your Divine Firebrand to spark us! Kindle in us belief in your promises! Ignite us to action! In your Son's name. Amen.

The sure meaning of Scripture! Well, then, let us abandon parables and figurative language and quote Christ's own simple, plainspoken, unembellished words:

I am the Way, the Truth and the Life;
No one can come to the Father except through me.
If you know me, you know my Father too.
From this moment you know him and have seen him. . . .

To have seen me is to have seen the Father, so how can you say, "Let us see the Father"? Do you not believe that I am in the Father and the Father is in me? The words I say to you I do not speak as from myself: it is the Father, living in me, who is doing this work. You must believe me when I say that I am in the Father and the Father is in

50

me; believe it on the evidence of this work, if for no other reason. I tell you most solemnly, whoever believes in me will perform the same works as I do myself; he will perform even greater works (John 14:6-12 JB).

Nor let us forget that very plain-speaking Christ-follower, Paul.

You are God's chosen race, his saints; he loves you, and you should be clothed in sincere compassion, in kindness and humility, gentleness and patience. Bear with one another; forgive each other as soon as a quarrel begins. The Lord has forgiven you; now you must do the same (Col. 3:12-13 JB).

No Christian will deny that Christ is the Way, the Truth, and the Life, or that Christ's Way, his Truth, his Life is the Way, the Truth, and the Life of forgiving love. Or that it is God's will and intention that the Way, the Truth, and the Life of forgiving love be our Way, our Truth, our Life. Having unconditionally given us the condition of forgiveness through his Son Jesus Christ, he intends us to exercise it in our lives. He intends our forgiveness to deepen our consciousness of sin and heighten our willingness to put on the Christlike disposition to forgive. He intends his forgiveness to make us see that we minimize what Christ has done for us by not incarnating forgiveness in our own lives. But the God of the new covenant does not reveal his intention to us with thunder and lightning. Indeed, it is his very gentle reticence about his forgiveness that quickens our consciousness of sin and our spirit of forgiveness (once again the dialectical movement of the spirit, the downward/upward, upward/downward movement of spirit!). P. T. Forsythe is amazingly insightful on this particular point.

> You find poor human creatures who never can overlook your mistake without conveying to you that it is as much as they can do. They think no little of themselves for doing it. They take care that you shall never forget their magnanimity in doing it. They keep the cost of their forgiveness ever before you. And the result is that it is not forgiveness at all. How miserable a thing it is instead! How this spirit takes the charm from the reconciliation! How it destroys the grace of it! How penurious the heart it betrays! How it shrivels the magnanimity it parades! How grudging, how ungodlike it is! How unfatherly! What an ungracious way of dealing with the graceless!
> That is not God's way of forgiveness. His Fatherhood has the grand manner. It has not only distinction but delicacy. He leaves us *to find out* in great measure what it cost—slowly, with the quickened heart of the forgiven, to find that out. . . . So gracious is God with his revelation that he actually lets it come home to us as if we had discovered it. This is his fine manner—so to give as if we had found.

At this point it is best to return to the story of the prodigal son. After all, it came first from the mouth of our Lord before it was written down and became Scripture. Moreover, our Lord told it with the intention to provide us with "the sure meaning" of our Father's love. P. T. Forsythe's insights into the parable of the prodigal son in *The Holy Father and the Living Christ* match Søren Kierkegaard's.

> What would you think of the forgiven son, who as the pardoned years went on never took his mercy seriously

enough to give a thought to what he had brought on his father or God? If he never cared to go behind that free forgiveness which met him and feasted him without an upbraiding word, if he never sought to look deep into those eyes which had followed him, watched him, and spied him so far. If he were never moved by the amazing welcome to put himself in the depths of his Father's place, if he took it all with a light heart, and told the world that in forgiveness he felt nothing but gladness; if he said that was all we know and all we need to know; if the swift forgiveness of God made it easy for him to forgive himself and just forget his past, if the generous, patient father never became for him the Holy Father, if he felt it was needless and fruitless to enter into the dread depths of sin with the altar candle of the Lord, or explore the miracle of the Father's grace—what would you think of him then?

Give him, of course, a year or two, if need be, to revel in this glad and sweet surprise. Give to his soul (if need be) a honeymoon. But if the years go on and he shows no thirst to search those things which the angels desire to look into but cannot (being unhuman and unredeemed), if he never seeks to measure the latent meaning of it all from the Redeemer, and gives no sign of being deepened in conscience as the fruit of being redeemed there; if there be no trace of coming to himself in a sense still deeper than when he was among the swine; if he go on with a mere readiness of religious emotion, and a levity of religious intelligence which cares not to measure his sin by the finer standards of the Father's spirit, or gauge the holy severity of the love he spurned; if he learns nothing of the Lord's controversy and his mortal moral strife; if he weighs nothing of the sin of the world on the scales of eternal redemption—if his career in grace were such as that what should we think of him then?

So far P. T. Forsythe. To balance the dialectical movement of the spirit, I continue in the same vein—but upward, toward the heightening of the spirit of forgiveness, which in another sense may be a coming-down-again movement, a coming back down to live forgiveness as the law of our forgiven being, to discover what the Spirit of forgiveness can accomplish in us, to learn that God's forgiveness cannot be cooped up in our own hearts. If it does not go out in forgiving love to others, there is an emptiness in the human spirit where God desires fruits and the fullness thereof.

What would you think of the forgiven son who the day after the banquet, the day after a good night's sleep on a stomach full of fatted calf, once again looked upon his father as a tiresome old man who had never traveled to foreign countries and did not know what life was like out there in the real world? Who once again could not forgive his father for his old-fashioned ideas and outmoded morals and obsolete orthodoxy. What if the forgiven prodigal overheard his brother upbraiding his father for making a feast on his behalf and never forgave his brother for the hardness of his heart—indeed, for the rest of his life found his prime joy in provoking and persecuting his brother, stern son of duty, Mr. Morality in person. What if six months after the Prodigal's return home a woman from his prodigal past came big with his child to his father's house, seeking shelter for herself and her unborn child, and he drove her away, furious that she dared reappear in his life, fearful that she might interfere with his coming marriage to the lovely respectable daughter of the wealthy mayor of the nearby city? What if he was irritable with his mother because she could not love the girl he planned to marry (no woman is ever good enough for a mother's son!), and after his marriage never brought his wife and their children to his parental house, although he did bring them to her funeral many years later and filled a pew with her grandchildren. What if his own firstborn son came to him on his 18th birthday and asked for a share of his inheritance because he could not wait until the old man was dead, and he gave his firstborn son his inheritance and told him to get out and never darken his door again. The son did go away, spent his inheritance on a life of debauchery, wined and dined and womanized. When he had spent his last penny and his friends, even the prostitutes, had abandoned him, he went home to his father's house. But his father met him at the door, cursed him, and shut the door in his face.

What would you think of the prodigal son then? Would we not have reason to believe that the prodigality of his heart and spirit was far more corrupting than the prodigality of his flesh? Would we not have reason to doubt that the forgiven son had ever truly opened his heart and spirit to the truth of his father's forgiveness? Could we not safely assume that he never crossed the frontier from the land of tit for tat, like for like, where cause and effect are the law of the land, where the slapped slap back and the libeled sue and the victim retaliates? Could we not assume that he never moved into the state of forgiveness, where forgiveness is the law of the spirit, as fundamental a law in the realm of the human spirit as the law of gravity is fundamental in the world of nature?

If we break the law of gravity, we break an arm, a leg, a neck, a back. If we break the law of forgiveness, we sow the seeds of hatred in the world and increase its disunity. If we break the law of forgiveness, we break the peace, we break community. But that is not all that happens! If we break the law of forgiveness, we inflict a mortal wound on our own spirits. We become our own greatest enemy and injure our own selves far more than the unfriends and enemies we cannot forgive. Who did it? Who sabotaged my inner being? I—I—I! I did it!

The sure meaning of Scripture is that there is forgiveness of sins for sinners. The sure meaning of Scripture is that Christ is the Way, the Truth, and the Life. The sure meaning of Scripture is that the Way is the way of forgiving love; the Truth is the truth of forgiving love, and the Life is the life of forgiving love. To receive God's forgiveness through his Son Christ is to receive the Truth, the Way, and the Life—and become a different person. It means to become new, *to change*.

"Oh, but I was changed!" William James reported a farmer to have said when he suddenly understood the message of Scripture. "I was changed, and everything became new. My horses and hogs and even everybody seemed changed!" One can be quite sure that the changed farmer changed in his treatment of his horses and hogs as well as of his fellow human beings!

 7

Change Is the Miracle

One of the Pharisees asked him to eat with him, and he went into the Pharisee's house, and took his place at table. And behold, a woman of the city, who was a sinner, when she learned that he was at table in the Pharisee's house, brought an alabaster flask of ointment, and standing behind him at his feet, weeping, she began to wet his feet with her tears, and wiped them with the hair of her head, and kissed his feet, and anointed them with the ointment.

Now when the Pharisee who had invited him saw it, he said to himself, "If this man were a prophet, he would have known who and what sort of woman this is who is touching him, for she is a sinner." And Jesus answering said to him, "Simon, I have something to say to you." And he answered, "What is it, Teacher?"

"A certain creditor had two debtors; one owed 500 denarii, and the other fifty. When they could not pay, he forgave them both. Now which of them will love him more?" Simon answered, "The one, I suppose, to whom he forgave more." And he said to him, "You have judged rightly."

Then turning toward the woman he said to Simon, "Do you see this woman? I entered your house, you gave me no water for my feet, but she has wet my feet with her tears and wiped them with her hair. You gave me no kiss, but from the time I came in she has not ceased to kiss my feet. You did not anoint my head with oil, but she has anointed my feet with ointment. Therefore I tell you, her sins, which are many, are forgiven, for she loved much; but he who is forgiven little, loves little." And he said to her, "Your sins are forgiven." Then those who were at table with him began to say among themselves, "Who is this, who even forgives sins?" And he said to the woman, "Your faith has saved you; go in peace."

Luke 7:36-50

Prayer Meditation

You Spirit of Holiness, you live in our unholiness.
You Spirit of Wisdom, you live in our unwisdom.
You Spirit of Truth, you live in our untruth.

Oh, please stay there! You have every right to go looking for a more desirable address, but you do not do so. After all, it would be a futile search! You, who are creating and regenerating and making your own house, oh, keep on living here so that some day you may be pleased with the house you are making in my unworthy heart.

Søren Kierkegaard

No, no, you and I do not *have to change* in order to move into the state of forgiveness! The state of forgiveness, which is to receive the forgiveness of sins from Christ in faith, does the changing and makes for newness.

The news in our daily papers is stale the minute we have

58

read it. But *this* news is never stale. It cannot be repeated enough. It cannot be overemphasized.

Forgiveness of sins is the great renewal Christ has brought into the world.

Forgiveness of sins is the new life Christ has brought into the world.

Forgiveness of sins is the new relationship to God Christ has brought into the world.

Forgiveness of sins is the new relationship to others Christ has brought into the world.

Sometimes I wish that the gospel writers had told us what happened to the woman who was a sinner and the woman caught in the act of adultery *after* Christ forgave their sins. Then again I am happy that they did not tell us, for I can let my imagination dance with those two women. I can walk up to the Lord's table with my fellow respectables and imagine them at the head of the procession, leading all of us who lead such good decent lives. Believing in the forgiveness of their sins, adoring their Savior, they walk as buoyantly as if there were no law of gravity. Indeed, they are as light as a bird! For what is more *up*lifting, asks Kierkegaard— the thought of our own good deeds or the thought of God's grace and mercy?

"A new kingdom has been established," wrote Cardinal Newman in *Plain Sermons.* Meditating on Matt. 19:30— "Many that are first shall be last, and the last shall be first"— Newman described the new kingdom as "not merely different from all kingdoms before it, but contrary to them, a paradox in the eyes of man—the visible rule of the invisible Savior."

Who reads Victor Hugo's 750-page novel, *Les Miserables,* anymore? Perhaps it would be read if *Reader's Digest* would gobble up enough paragraphs to reduce the book to 100 pages. But that would ruin the most beautiful story in literature of "what happened afterward"—after the great event of forgiveness.

The great event of forgiveness takes place on page 106. Jean Valjean, who had just been released from the galleys after serving 19 years for breaking a pane of glass in a bakery and stealing a loaf of bread for his widowed sister and her seven starving children, was refused food and shelter at every inn and hostel because of his yellow passport, identifying him as a criminal. Finally he was sent to the bishop's house and was invited by the bishop to come in.

He came in, took one step, and paused, leaving the door open behind him. He had his knapsack on his back, his stick in his hand, and a rough, hard, tired, and fierce look in his eyes, as seen by the firelight. He was hideous. It was an apparition of ill omen.

Mme. Magloire [the housekeeper] had not even the strength to scream. She stood trembling with her mouth open.

Mdlle. Baptistine [the bishop's sister] turned, saw the man enter and started out half alarmed; then slowly turning back again toward the fire, she looked at her brother, and her face resumed its usual calmness and serenity.

The bishop looked upon the man with a tranquil eye.

As he was opening his mouth to speak, doubtless to ask the stranger what he wanted, the man, leaning with both hands on his club, glanced from one to another in turn, and, without waiting for the bishop to speak, said, in a loud voice:

"See here! My name is Jean Valjean. I am a convict; I have been nineteen years in the galleys. Four days ago I was set free, and started for Pontarlier, which is my destination; during these four days I have walked from Toulon. Today I have walked twelve leagues. When I reached this place this evening I went to an inn, and they sent me away on account of my yellow passport, which I had shown at the mayor's office, as was necessary. I went to another inn; they said: 'Get out!' It was the same with one as with another; nobody would have me. I went to the prison and the turnkey would not let me in. I crept into a dog kennel, the dog bit me, and drove me away as if he had been a man; you would have said that he knew who I was. I went into the fields to sleep beneath the stars; there were no stars. I thought it would rain, and there was no good God to stop the drops, so I came back to the town to get the shelter of some doorway. There in the square I laid down upon a stone; a good woman showed me your house, and said: 'Knock there!' I have knocked. What is this place? Are you an inn? I have money, my savings; 109 francs and 15 sous, which I have earned in the galleys by my work for nineteen years. I will pay. What do I care? I have money. I am very tired—twelve leagues on foot—and I am so hungry. Can I stay?"

"Mme. Magloire," said the bishop, "put on another plate."

The man took three steps and came near the lamp which stood on the table. "Stop," he exclaimed; as if he had not been understood; "not that, did you understand me? I am a galley slave—a convict—I am just from the galleys." He drew from his pocket a large sheet of yellow paper, which he unfolded. "There is my passport, yellow, as you see. That is enough to have me kicked out wherever I go. Will you read it? I know how to read, I do. I learned it in the galleys. There is a school there for those who care for it. See, here is what they have put in

my passport: 'Jean Valjean, a liberated convict, native of
_____,' you don't care for that, 'has been nineteen years
in the galleys; five years for burglary; fourteen years for
having attempted four times to escape. This man is very
dangerous.' There you have it! Everybody has thrust me
out; will you receive me? Is this an inn? Can you give me
something to eat and a place to sleep? Have you a sta-
ble?"

"Mme. Magloire," said the bishop, "put some sheets on
the bed in the alcove."

At the bishop's gentle insistence, the housekeeper set the
table with the silver plates and the silver candlesticks. The
convict ate greedily. Later he was shown to a bed with clean
sheets, but he was so exhausted that he fell upon it fully
dressed and slept soundly. However, unused to a soft bed,
he awakened at two o'clock. He began to think, and the
bitter thoughts of how society had robbed him and seemingly would continue to rob him even though he had been
freed led him to steal the silver plates, put them in his
knapsack, run across the garden, leap over the wall, and
flee.

The theft was discovered in the morning by the housekeeper. As she went back and forth serving the bishop and
his sister, her mind was filled with I-told-you-so thoughts.

"Was there ever such an idea?" said Mme. Magloire to
herself as she went backward and forward; "to take in a
man like that, and to give him a bed beside; and yet what
a blessing it was he did nothing but steal! Oh, my stars!
it makes the chills run over me when I think of it!"

Just as the brother and sister were rising from the table
there was a knock at the door.

"Come in," said the bishop.

The door opened. A strange, fierce group appeared on the threshold. Three men were holding a fourth by the collar. The three men were gendarmes; the fourth, Jean Valjean.

A brigadier of gendarmes, who appeared to head the group, was near the door. He advanced toward the bishop, giving a military salute:

"Monseigneur," said he.

At this word Jean Valjean, who was sullen, and seemed entirely cast down, raised his head with a stupified air.

"Monseigneur!" he murmured, "then it is not the curé!"

"Silence!" said a gendarme, "it is Monseigneur, the bishop."

In the meantime Mgr. Bienvenu had approached as quickly as his great age permitted.

"Ah, there you are!" said he, looking toward Jean Valjean, "I am glad to see you. But I gave you the candlesticks also, which are silver like the rest, and would bring 200 francs. Why did you not take them along with your plates?"

Jean Valjean opened his eyes and looked at the bishop with an expression which no human tongue could describe.

"Monseigneur," said the brigadier, "then what the man said was true? We met him. He was going like a man who was running away, and we arrested him in order to see. He had this silver."

"And he told you," interrupted the bishop, with a smile, "that it had been given him by a good old priest with whom he had passed the night. I see it all. And you brought him back here? It is all a mistake."

"If that is so," said the brigadier, "we can let him go."

"Certainly," replied the bishop.

The gendarmes released Jean Valjean, who shrank back.

"Is it true that they let me go?" he said in a voice almost inarticulate, as if he were speaking in his sleep.

"Yes! you can go. Do you not understand?" said a gendarme.

"My friend," said the bishop, "before you go away here are your candlesticks; take them."

He went to the mantelpiece, took the two candlesticks and brought them to Jean Valjean. The two women beheld the action without a word, or gesture, or look that might disturb the bishop.

Jean Valjean was trembling in every limb. He took the two candlesticks mechanically and with a wild appearance.

"Now," said the bishop, "go in peace. By the way, my friend, when you come again you need not come through the garden. You can always come in and go out by the front door. It is closed only with a latch, day or night."

Then turning to the gendarmes, he said:

"Messieurs, you can retire." The gendarmes withdrew. Jean Valjean felt like a man who is just about to faint. The bishop approached him and said, in a low voice: "Forget not, never forget that you have promised me to use this silver to become an honest man."

Jean Valjean, who had no recollection of this promise, stood confounded. The bishop had laid much stress upon these words as he uttered them. He continued, solemnly:

"Jean Valjean, my brother, you belong no longer to evil, but to good. It is your soul that I am buying for you. I withdraw it from dark thoughts and from the spirit of perdition and I give it to God!"

The rest of the novel, the remaining 644 pages, describes Jean Valjean's reponse to the bishop's great act of forgiveness. He who 19 years before had entered the galleys in despair and came out sullen and bitter now experienced the miracle of change. The bishop's forgiveness created a break with his past, and he walked out into a new life, changed in mind, changed in attitude, changed in heart. If he had not experienced this event of forgiveness, he might have tried to forget his act of betrayal of the gentle old man, but his act of betrayal would have persisted in remembering him. His despair would have been compounded, perhaps to madness, certainly to desperate acts that would have placed him once again in chains.

Someone has said that revenge is the natural, automatic response to insult, injury, and wrong. It is expected and can be calculated. But forgiveness is unexpected, incalculable, and unpredictable. And so it is, anywhere and everywhere outside the state of forgiveness. Revenge is the old story, as old as the history of fallen humanity. It was to be predicted, indeed, it was inevitable that Jean Valjean would wreak his hopeless despair and rage on society and end up this time on the gallows instead of in the galleys. But the shock of the bishop's forgiveness broke the old chain of cause and effect, and he suddenly found himself in a *new* state, the state in which the gentle old bishop lived, the state where forgiveness is the law of the land, the law of the spirit. Jean Valjean did not have to change to enter the state of forgiveness. His entering the state of forgiveness through a great act of forgiveness changed Jean Valjean.

8

More Miracles—Some Scriptural, Some Fictional

And when they came to the place which is called The Skull, there they crucified him, and the criminals, one on the right and one on the left. And Jesus said, "Father, forgive them; for they know not what they do."

Luke 23:33-34

Then they cast him out of the city and stoned him; and the witnesses laid down their garments at the feet of a young man named Saul. And as they were stoning Stephen, he prayed, "Lord Jesus, receive my spirit." And he knelt down and cried with a loud voice, "Lord, do not hold this sin against them." And when he had said this, he fell asleep.

Acts 7:58-60

Prayer Meditation

Note left behind by a Jewish prisoner in a concentration camp:

Peace to all men of evil will. Let there be an end to all demands for punishment and retribution.

67

Crimes have surpassed all measure. They can no longer be grasped by human understanding. There are too many martyrs.

And so lay not these sufferings on the scale of justice, Lord, and lay not these sufferings on the torturers' charge, to exact a terrible reckoning for them.

Pay them back in a different way. Put down in favor of the executioners, the informers, the traitors, and all men of evil will the courage, the spiritual strength of the others, the humility, their lofty dignity, their constant inner striving and invincible hope, the souls that staunched the tears, their love, their ravaged broken hearts that remained steadfast and confident in the face of death itself—yes, even at moments of utmost weakness.

Let all this, O Lord, be laid before thee for the forgiveness of sins as a ransom for the triumph of righteousness.

Let the good and not the evil be taken into account.

And may we remain in our enemies' memory not as their victims, not as a nightmare, not as a haunting spectre, but as helpers in their striving to destroy the fury of their criminal passions.

There is nothing more we want of them, and when it is all over grant us to live among men as men and may peace come again to our poor earth—peace for men of goodwill and for all others.

When we say that the state of forgiveness is a brand-new state, we do not say that forgiveness did not exist prior to Christ's coming to earth. There are great acts of forgiveness

recorded in the Old Testament just as there are great n~
acts. An example of a tragic non-act of forgiveness
Sarah's refusal to forgive Hagar for bearing Abraham
even though Sarah in her barrenness had borrowed
speak, Hagar's womb to produce a son and heir for Ab
It is a poignant scene of powerful human emotions i

Indeed, it surprises me that this story has not
in any Sunday school curriculum that I have seen—
of the feast Abraham and Sarah gave on the da
weaned. How old was he? Perhaps two or three years old.
At least he was running around and playing with his half
brother when Sarah's eyes fell on the two of them. Imagine
the scene. Sarah was walking around, surveying the guests
eating their full of lamb roasted to perfection, dates fresh
and juicy and plump. Sarah was immensely satisfied, knowing that this party would go down on the social records as
the party of the year—perhaps even of the decade! Then she
saw the son of Hagar the Egyptian playing with her own
son Isaac. She called Abraham to her and said, "Cast out
this slave woman with her son; for the son of this slave
woman shall not be heir with my son Isaac."

Do you hear Sarah's despising, rejecting words echoing
down through the ages?

"Drive the Indians out! Put them on reservations. The
Indians shall not own this land!"

"Place the blacks in South Africa on tribal reserves. This
is our land, and apartheid is our policy."

"No blacks (or Indians) served here."

"Not on your life, no group home for the retarded in our
neighborhood!"

"No Hmong refugees from Southeast Asia are welcome in our community!"

"Germany for the pure Aryans! Wipe out the Jewish race!"

"The West Bank of the Jordan belongs to the Jews. Arabs are not welcome!"

We cannot help wondering if everything would have been different in the Near East if Sarah had forgiven Hagar and Ishmael. Would the miracle have happened? Would the descendants of Ishmael be living at peace with the descendants of Isaac today instead of being constantly at the point of war?

On the bright and forgiving side of human history in the Old Testament, we have the forgiveness scene in which Esau forgave Jacob. In Gen. 27:41 we read: "Now Esau hated Jacob because of the blessing with which his father had blessed him, and Esau said to himself, 'The days of mourning for my father are approaching; then I will kill my brother Jacob.'" Rebekah cautioned Jacob to flee to Laban, her brother in Haran. Jacob did so, and again by native shrewdness prospered. Years later he returned with two wives, numerous children, many servants, and much livestock. But he returned in fear of his brother's vengeance.

"But Esau ran to meet him, and embraced him, and fell on his neck and kissed him, and they wept." How that miracle happened, we are not told.

Another great forgiveness scene is in the novel *Joseph and His Brothers* tucked into the book of Genesis. Indeed, the novel is all about forgiveness, climaxing in the scene in which Joseph sent all the Egyptians from the room and made himself known to his brothers.

70

"And he wept aloud, so that the Egyptians heard it, and the household of Pharaoh heard it. And Joseph said to his brothers, 'I am Joseph; is my father still alive?' "

Joseph had a hard time convincing his brothers that he had truly forgiven them and that they had nothing to fear. In fact, years later, after their father had died in Egypt and had been buried "back home" in Abraham's burial place, the brothers feared that Joseph would now "pay them back."

When Joseph's brothers saw that their father was dead, they said, "It may be that Joseph will hate us and pay us back for all the evil which we did to him." So they sent a message to Joseph, saying, "Your father gave this command before he died, 'Say to Joseph, Forgive, I pray you, the transgressions of your brothers and their sin, because they did evil to you.' And now, we pray you, forgive the transgression of the servants of the God of your father." Joseph wept when they spoke to him. His brothers also came and fell down before him, and said, "Behold, we are your servants." But Joseph said to them, "Fear not, for am I in the place of God? As for you, you meant evil against me; but God meant it for good, to bring it about that many people should be kept alive, as they are today. So do not fear; I will provide for you and your little ones." Thus he reassured them and comforted them (Gen. 50:15-21).

Yes, there are great scenes of forgiveness in the Old Testament, but they are isolated scenes. Nowhere is forgiveness a way of life, a principle of being, the basis for human relationships, the law that governs conduct, the condition for citizenship in a state. That their God was unlike any other god, totally different from the gods of the Philistines and the Egyptians and that he was uniquely a God of forgiveness, this the Israelites knew. After all, he repeatedly called them through their prophets to repentance and the constancy of *his* forgiveness. He forgave their backslidings and rebellions again and again.

> The Lord is merciful and gracious,
> slow to anger and abounding in steadfast love.
> He will not always chide,
> nor will he keep his anger for ever.
> He does not deal with us according to our sins,
> nor requite us according to our iniquities.
> For as the heavens are high above the earth,
> so great is his steadfast love
> toward those who fear him.
> For he knows our frame;
> he remembers that we are dust (Ps. 103:8-15).

> Though your sins are like scarlet, they shall be white as snow (Isa. 1:18).

> . . . for I will forgive their iniquity, and I will remember their sin no more (Jer. 31:34).

> Who is a God like thee, pardoning iniquity
> and passing over transgression
> for the remnant of his inheritance?
> He does not retain his anger for ever
> because he delights in steadfast love.
> He will again have compassion upon us,
> he will tread our iniquities under foot.
> Thou wilt cast all our sins
> into the depths of the sea (Mic. 7:18-19).

When we speak of Christ's miracles in the New Testament, we often neglect to rank the forgiveness of our sins as his greatest miracle. When we speak of forgiveness of sins in Christ Jesus, we often fail to include that he *also* calls us to forgive as we are forgiven and to form a redemptive community, a state of forgiveness *here and now.* We too are called to perform miracles of forgiveness—and not occasionally, not conditionally, not spasmodically, not capriciously. In the state of forgiveness one is predisposed and prepared at all times to perform the miracle of forgiveness.

Not so strangely, in literature it is more often women who perform miracles of forgiveness and redeem the prodigals they love. In Ibsen's play *Peer Gynt,* Solveig, whose way was the way of forgiveness and love, waited a lifetime for Peer Gynt, whose way was the way of the troll, "to yourself, be enough." When he returned at last, he was aged, burned out, and fully aware that his soul was a shriveled fetus. "Where has Peer Gynt been all these years?" he cried to Solveig. "In my faith, in my hope, and in my love," she answered. In Solveig's forgiving arms the miracle happened, and the rising of the sun leads us to believe that Peer Gynt at long last was on the way to becoming a self.

In Dostoevski's *Crime and Punishment,* it is Sonia whose constant forgiving love finally broke through the hard crust of Raskolnikov's superman notion that he was beyond good and evil. But not until the epilog! His surrendering to the law late in the novel was not done in repentance for having murdered an old pawnbroker woman to prove his philosophy. "Crime, what crime?" he said. "I killed a vile noxious insect, an old pawnbroker woman of no use to anyone."

Even when Sonia followed him to Siberia, where he served out his sentence, he did not repent his crime, and he tortured her with his indifference to her presence in the village and to her visits. The miracle did not happen until after a long illness he unexpectedly met Sonia on the river bank, where he had been sent under guard to work. Sonia gave him a joyful smile of welcome and held out her hand. Previously he had taken her hand as though with repugnance.

How it happened he did not know. But all at once something seemed to seize him and fling him at her feet. He wept and threw his arms round her knees. For the first instant she was terribly frightened and she turned pale. She jumped up and looked at him trembling. But at the same moment she understood, and a light of infinite happiness came into her eyes. She knew and had no doubt that he loved her beyond everything and that at last the moment had come. . . .

They wanted to speak, but could not; tears stood in their eyes. They were both pale and thin; but those sick pale faces were bright with the dawn of a new future, of a full resurrection into a new life. They were renewed by love; the heart of each held infinite sources of life for the heart of the other.

They resolved to wait and be patient. They had another seven years to wait, and what terrible suffering and what infinite happiness before them! But he had risen again and he knew it and felt it in all his being, while she—she only lived in his life.

On the evening of the same day, when the barracks were locked, Raskolnikov lay on his plank bed and thought of her. He had even fancied that day that all the convicts who had been his enemies looked at him differently; he had even entered into talk with them and they answered him in a friendly way. He remembered that now, and thought it was bound to be so. Wasn't everything now bound to be changed?

In Alan Paton's powerful novel *Cry, the Beloved Country* the miracle of forgiveness was performed by a white man and a black man. The Zulu pastor's prodigal son Absalom had entered a house in a suburb of Johannesburg with the intent to steal but not to kill. Frightened by the house-holder, whom he did not expect to be at home, he shot him. The murder was especially tragic because the victim had been a great fighter for racial justice in South Africa and was the son of a well-known and highly respected farmer in the fertile highground above the black pastor's poor erod-ed parish. The murderer was apprehended, tried, and sen-tenced to be hanged. The paths of the two bereaved fathers crossed—as well as the paths of the aged Zulu pastor and the murdered man's young son "with the brightness inside of him." Prior to this tragedy, James Jarvis, the father of the murdered man, had not questioned the injustices of the South African system. His search to understand his dead son's liberal views and his encounter with Kumalo, the Zulu pastor, opened his eyes and heart to the plight of rural and urban Africans. A man of enclosed reserve, he nevertheless sensed and understood the sufferings of the black pastor whose son had murdered his own son. As a memorial to his son, he decided to give practical help to Kumalo's drought-stricken village and to rebuild his church.

Like *Cry, the Beloved Country*, Alan Paton's novel *Too Late the Phalarope* summons us to "turn to the holy task of pardon, that the body of the Lord might not be wounded twice."

Perhaps it is not strange that torn and anguished South Africa has produced another great writer who hammers on

75

our souls with his novels of suffering and forgiveness. Laurens van der Post's *The Seed and the Sower* is a story of the harvest of pain in the seedbed of the heart that a seemingly trifling betrayal can grow. *Seemingly* trifling, said Celliers, who wrote his story on coarse yellow sheets of toilet paper in a Japanese prison camp in Java during World War II.

> I had a brother once and I betrayed him. The betrayal in itself was so slight that most people would find "betrayal" too exaggerated a word, and think me morbidly sensitive for so naming it. . . . I can assure you that one of the most significant characteristics of betrayal is that it is neither spectacular nor presumptuous in origin. Indeed, those treacheries destined to reach farthest in their consequences prefer not to be obvious or dramatic in their beginnings but rather to wait, humbly and unostentatiously, until they are ready to bear their bitter fruit in maturity. They seem to favour presenting themselves to the unguarded heart selected to become their own private seedbed as trivialities in the daily routine of life, as insignificant occurrences so self-evident that no question of a choice and so no choice of rejection arises out of their appearance on the familiar scene of everyday events. In fact betrayal behaves as if it were worth no more than the miserable thirty pieces of silver that were paid for the greatest and most meaningful betrayal of all time.

The betrayal was the older brother's pretending that he had not witnessed and was unaware of his classmates' cruel, sadistic initiation of his younger hunchbacked brother—dunking him, stripping off his shirt, exposing his hunch, jeering, screaming. When Celliers saw his brother in the evening he said with gay nonchalance, "How did you get on today?"

"Then you weren't there?" His question was flat.

"Not where?" I answered, seeking respite in evasion.

"At the round-up [the initiation]." He peered at me in the twilight.

"Oh, there!" I replied easily. "No, I was in the science lab most of the afternoon. Had a job for the Science master to do. In fact, I've just now finished.

Over the years, the betrayal continued to yield its harvest in the seedbeds of both hearts. "That is another aspect of betrayals. It has a will of its own which feeds on the very will that seeks to deny it. I might have succeeded in forgetting the event if it had not so obstinately persisted in remembering me."

Celliers became a successful lawyer, but a strange nothingness grew in his soul. "At the time, of course, I did not understand this sabotage of the invisible dimensions of my being. That came about only many years later. So I became a sufferer denied even the comfort of knowing the name of his disease; and that feeling of uncertainty promptly planted its own colony of uneasiness on the mainland of my spirit."

World War II came, offering Celliers escape from the nothingness that had invaded his spirit. In North Africa, he became more and more skilled at raiding and killing and volunteered for every hazardous operation behind enemy lines. Finally he was sent on a special mission to Palestine to train cutthroat raiders and found himself stationed in a monastery. Through his encounter with a monk and through a vision he understood at last that the real war was within him, not without, and that it had begun years before when he had betrayed his hunchbacked younger brother. After an attack of malaria, Celliers used his month's convalescent leave to make the long journey back to South Africa and his brother's farm.

"So I went straight to the heart of the matter and told him I had come to tell him of a great wrong I had once done and to ask his forgiveness."

His brother had known it all the time.

"You knew?"
He nodded. "But now we're free of it all, thanks to you."

But this is not the end of the story, and this is not the only forgiveness scene in *The Seed and the Sower*. Because Celliers could speak Dutch, he was sent to Southeast Asia, where he was captured, tortured, and starved by his captors and finally brought, barely alive, to a prison camp in Java under the notorious Japanese commander Yonoi. By this time the Japanese commanders foresaw defeat, and the dimension of despair was electric in the atmosphere of their prison camps. Yonoi had been trying to force the prisoners to identify the armament experts and gunsmiths among them, but they chose to lie and tell him that there were not any.

One day, shortly after Celliers' arrival in the prison camp, Yonoi ordered all prisoners, also the sick and dying, to assemble on the parade ground. The entire encampment of Japanese soldiers, fully armed, surrounded them and set up machine guns at each corner of the parade ground. After making the prisoners stand for one hour in the blazing sun, Yonoi appeared and came straight to the center of the parade ground. He summoned Hicksley-Ellis, the spokesman of the English prisoners. Through an interpreter Yonoi asked how many armament experts and gunsmiths he had in the camp. Hicksley-Ellis answered, "None."

Then, Yonoi, being what he was, cracked inside. He had Hicksley-Ellis tied with his hands behind his back and made to kneel bareheaded on the ground near him. Yonoi then stepped back, drew his sword, raised it flashing in the sun and with his lips to the naked steel said a prayer to it as I had seen other officers do before other executions. The machine gun crews released their safety catches and all four guns clicked loudly as they rammed the first bullet into the firing breech. One by one the heads would fall until someone broke—and even then it would not be the end.

It was then that Celliers broke out of the rank of prisoners and approached Yonoi, placing himself between Hicksley-Ellis and the Japanese commander. He said something quietly to Yonoi, who shrieked, "You—go back, back, back!"

Celliers shook his head quietly and went on staring at him steadily as a disarmed hunter might stare a growling lion straight in the face. Perhaps more in terror than in anger Yonoi raised his sword and knocked Celliers down with the flat of it. The crack on his head rang out like a pistol-shot, to be followed by another exhortation to Celliers to go back. Dazed, Celliers struggled to his feet, swayed and half turned as if to obey—then swung around suddenly. He took a couple of steps back toward Yonoi, put his hands on Yonoi's arms and embraced him on both cheeks rather like a French general embracing a soldier after a decoration for valor.

Yonoi was stunned, but his officers, feeling that their commander had been insulted, suddenly uttered the "an-

79

thropoidal yell which always preceded a Japanese bayonet charge," jumped forward, and proceeded to beat Celliers insensible and unrecognizable except for his yellow hair. Yonoi finally halted the beating. Because Yonoi had lost face, a new commander took over the command of the camp. Three days later, the prisoners were ordered to dig a hole in the center of the parade ground, and the barely conscious Celliers was buried up to his neck and left under guard, with no food or water, to die. Before that happened, at three o'clock in the morning, Yonoi suddenly appeared, sent away the Japanese guards, bent down, and with a scissors snipped a strand of yellow hair from the dying man's head. For some time he remained there in deep thought, then bowed low to Celliers and walked to the gate to summon the guards. He was never seen in the prison camp again.

However, after the war and during the war trials, a former prisoner and now an interpreter at the trials recognized Yonoi. Fearing that he would be hanged and would be unable to fulfill his burning mission in life, Yonoi gave the strand of yellow hair to the former prisoner and asked him to do what had to be done so that he, Yonoi, could die as he ought to die. But Yonoi was not hanged, and after four years in prison he was released. The former prisoner sent the strand of yellow hair from Celliers' head to Yonoi in Japan, where Yonoi carried the strand to the sacred shrine of his ancestors and dedicated it to the sacred fire of his people's shrine.

Forgiveness was unknown in Japanese culture. Unable to forgive his opponents, the Japanese man with superior power assassinated them. It was the expected thing to do. If a Japanese man failed to meet the intolerably high standards he or others had set for himself, he was unable to forgive himself and committed *hara-kiri*. It was the expected thing to do. By Celliers' unexpected act, Yonoi was shocked beyond code and culture to see himself and Celliers as two individuals. Years later when he presented himself at the shrine of his ancestors to dedicate the strand of Celliers' hair to the spirits, he bowed low, clapped his hands to let the spirits know that he was there, and deposited the poem he had written to them.

> In the spring,
> Obeying the August spirits
> I went to fight the enemy.
> In the fall,
> Returning I beg the spirits
> To receive also the enemy.

9

Ah, but the Pukahs!

So, then, if you are bringing your offering to the altar and there remember that your brother has something against you, leave your offering there before the altar, go and be reconciled with your brother first, and then come back and present your offering.

Matthew 5:23-24 JB

Speaking with God discovers us safely to ourselves. We *find* ourselves, come to ourselves, in the Spirit. Face your special weakness and sins before God. Force yourself to say to God exactly where you are wrong. When anything goes wrong, do not ask to have it set right without asking in prayer what it was in you that made it go wrong. It is somewhat pointless to ask for a general grace to help specific flaws, sins, trials, and griefs. Let prayer be actual, concrete, a direct product of life's real experiences. Pray as your actual self, not as some fancied saint. Let it be closely relevant to your real situation.

P. T. Forsythe, *The Soul of Prayer*

Prayer Meditation

"And forgive us our debts, as we also have forgiven our debtors" (Matt. 6:12).

Luther used a word for "stumbling block" that I wish could be adopted into the English language, especially to describe the "Yes, but" that we say when we are backing away from a yes and actually are saying no. It is the word *pukah*. In his exposition of the book of Genesis, Luther said,

> When the pastor of the church or some other servant of the Word comes to the aid of a distressed person and comforts his conscience, still, no matter how greatly he has comforted it, a sigh returns involuntarily and despite all feeling of consolation, I know what happens to me when I recall how I have lived in the past. For although I know that my sins are forgiven me, yet this *pukah,* this stumbling block, continues to return. I cannot live without a sob, without shame and blushing. I exclaim: "Shame on you! What have you done!" I know I am not guilty of violating another's wife, of murder or similar enormouses. There the little dog of regret cannot bite me; but it does bite me because of other sins, even though my conscience has been hushed and the scar has healed.

The stumbling blocks, the pukahs to cheerful and bold confidence that my sins are forgiven, are several and block the entrance to the state of forgiveness. Here are just a few.

1. I cannot understand the forgiveness of sins; therefore I cannot believe it.

2. I can believe in the forgiveness of sins for everyone else, but not for myself.

3. I can accept God's forgiveness, but I cannot and I will not ever forgive myself.

4. There are some people I cannot forgive.

5. There are some people from whom I cannot receive forgiveness.

6. So I am forgiven, but what about my relapses into sin?

Does not the doctrine of the forgiveness of sins make it possible for me to sin my way merrily to salvation? We shall address these pukahs one by one.

Pukah 1.   I cannot understand the forgiveness of sins; therefore I cannot believe it.

Suppose that the prodigal son had said that to his father, had wriggled out of his embrace, turned on his heels, and gone back to the pigs. Would that be trusting or distrusting the father's forgiveness? Would it be honoring or dishonoring the father's love? Would it be true repentance or a new sin? Would it be true humility or brazen defiance? Would it be picking a quarrel with the father?

Suppose someone says to God's face: "No, there is no forgiveness of sins. Impossible!" Is this another way of saying, "God, I don't think you are big enough to deal with something as big as the world's sin!" Or, "I'm too intelligent to subscribe to something so absurd. Now, if you would come up with a scheme where we could work off our guilt—well, there would be some sense to that. In fact, we would rather work off our petty little sins than be insulted by your forgiveness, which forgives big sinners as well as us little ones and does not seem to differentiate between us." Or, "God, if you would call forgiveness of sins a paradox, maybe then we could believe in it. Calling something a paradox, believing in paradoxes, is quite the "in" thing, you know. But to believe in the simple forgiveness of sin—well, it is incomprehensible, and I do not believe what I cannot understand!"

Granted, it is the greatest mystery ever conceived, and only the divine mind could come up with it, knowing full well that the natural mind could not grasp it. It is indeed inconceivable by and to the human mind!

> But, as it is written, "What no eye has seen, nor ear heard, nor the heart of man conceived, what God has prepared for those who love him," God has revealed to us through the Spirit. For the Spirit searches everything, even the depths of God. For what person knows a man's thoughts except the spirit of the man which is in him? So also no one comprehends the thoughts of God except the Spirit of God. Now we have received not the spirit of the world, but the Spirit which is from God, that we might understand the gifts bestowed on us by God. And we impart this in words not taught by human wisdom but taught by the Spirit, interpreting spiritual truths to those who possess the Spirit. The unspiritual man does not receive the gifts of the Spirit of God, for they are folly to him, and he is not able to understand them because they are spiritually discerned (1 Cor. 2:9-14).

The forgiveness of sins is impossible for the human mind to believe. It is not for those whom the British missionary

C. J. Studd called "nibblers of the possible" but for "grab-bers of the impossible." It must be proclaimed, not ex-plained. It is *gospel*—good news. It is for faith and fools, not intelligence and wisdom. It is not for the competent, chock-full head but for the poor and needy heart.

Do I need the forgiveness of sins? My heart tells me, "Yes, oh yes!" Do I desire the forgiveness of sins? "With all my heart!" Then, says Paul, put your mind in your heart and look steadfastly at Christ, who is your forgiveness of sins. God's grace through him is stronger than your sin. And God has sent the spirit of his Son into your heart, there to perform another miracle—to change your despair and unbelief into the miraculous, the prodigious, the crazy cour-age to dare to believe the staggering proclamation of the forgiveness of your sins in Christ Jesus. Our faith rests on Jesus, and he was absolutely sure of the unconditional for-giveness of his Father. Our faith rests on Jesus, and he did not only proclaim forgiveness—he ate with publicans and sinners. Our faith rests on Jesus, who died on the cross for our forgiveness, who even in the agony of death asked for and trusted in his Father's forgiveness of his crucifiers.

Give up God's gift because I cannot understand it, even by a tremendous exertion of mind? Having been taken across the Red Sea of my sins by a miracle I cannot understand, should I choose to wander for 40 years in the wilderness of *no,* never entering the kingdom of *yes,* the state of forgive-ness? Should I choose to go on despairing of the forgiveness of my sins, believing it is impossible because it is incom-prehensible?

Hear the apostle Paul on this:

The Son of God, the Christ Jesus that we proclaimed among you. . . was never Yes and No: with him it was

always Yes, and however many the promises God made, the Yes to them all is in him. That is why it is "through him" that we answer Amen to the praise of God. Remember it is God himself who assures us all and you of the standing in Christ, and has anointed us, marking us with his seal and giving us the pledge, the Spirit, that we carry in our hearts (2 Cor. 1:18-22 JB).

How can Pukah 1 stand before the greatest three passions in heaven or on earth, in time or in eternity? (1) The passion of God to forgive, (2) the passion of Christ to redeem, (3) the passion of the Spirit to help us comprehend the gift of forgiveness, apprehend it, and make it actual in our time? Before these passions, Pukah 1 bows down in all humility and withdraws. One roadblock removed!

Pukah 2. I can believe in the forgiveness of sins for everyone else, but not for myself.

Aha, one of these "deep natures" who think it is a mark of spiritual depth to say, "I can believe in the forgiveness of sins for everyone else but not for myself." Yet such persons may be preferable to those who automatically think it is "others" who need to and can be forgiven, not themselves. People who ask others but never themselves, "Were you there when they crucified my Lord? Were you there when they nailed him on the tree? Were you there when they pierced him in the side? Were you there when they laid him in the tomb? Were you there when he rose from the dead? Were you there when he ascended on high?" People who tremble for others but never for themselves. People who point the finger of guilt at others. Who murdered a reputation by gossip? Who alienated a son by hardening his

88

heart against him? Who killed a congregation by a personal vendetta against the pastor? Who split a women's church group into factions over the issue of buying a dishwasher? Who sent a child sobbing to bed? "He—she—they—did it Lord. Not I, Lord! *They* need forgiveness, not I, Lord. *They* need to be forgiven so that they can live in forgiveness—not I, Lord!"

However, it is more often the case that this particular pukah is a roadblock for self-denouncers. Indeed, they may even torment themselves with the thought that they have committed the unforgiveable sin, the sin against the Holy Spirit. Perhaps the sin against the Holy Spirit is the pride with which they believe that forgiveness of sin is for everyone but themselves!

I know a man who prides himself on not having gained a pound since he was a trim teenager. I call this "pride of no flesh." Similarly, a person who is halted at the entrance to the state of forgiveness may be stopped by pride in his or her unworthiness. But the forgiveness of sins is not related either to one's worthiness or unworthiness. It is related to receiving or not receiving the forgiveness of sins.

Back to Paul again: "The Christ Jesus we proclaim among you. . . was never Yes and No." You cannot say yes to the forgiveness of everyone else's sins and no to the forgiveness of your own. That is making your own personal guilt more important than God's transcendence, grace, and gift. Indeed, you are making yourself guilty of a much more fearful sin—mistrusting God's grace and mercy. You are dishonoring God by doubting his infinite pardoning love *for you*. This case calls for a "You *shall!*" Hear Kierkegaard on this:

The eternal consolation in the doctrine of the forgiveness of sins is this: You shall believe it. For when the

anxious conscience begins with heavy thoughts, and it is as if they could never in all eternity be forgotten, then comes this: You shall forget. You *shall* stop thinking of your sin. Not only are you permitted to let it alone, not only do you dare pray God for permission to dare forget—no, you shall forget it, for you shall believe that your sins are forgiven.

If your spirit is still so adolescent and immature that it rebels at "You shalls" and "You shall nots"—well, then you may as well pitch your tent outside the border of the state of forgiveness, for it will, alas, be a never-never land for you.

Pukah 3. I can accept God's forgiveness, but I cannot and I will not ever forgive myself.

One wonders if this is a question of doubt or obstinacy! It sounds so high-minded and high-souled, but it is rather the height of conceit for people not to forgive themselves for what God has already forgiven them! But many people do indeed go to the Communion service carrying the weight of their sins, hear the gracious forgiveness of their sins pronounced, eat Christ's body and drink his blood, and go home again still carrying the same weight of sin (or even one sin heavier).

Kierkegaard said in a Communion discourse:

The gracious forgiveness of all your sins! Hear it rightly. Take it absolutely literally—the forgiveness of all your sins. Divinely understood, you ought to be able to go away from the altar as light as a newborn baby, upon whom nothing weighs heavily, thus even lighter of heart, provided much has weighed upon your heart. There is no one at the altar

90

who hangs on to your sins, not even the least little one,
no one—unless you yourself do it. So throw them all away,
and throw away the memory of them lest you hang on to
them in your memory. And throw away the memory that
you have thrown your sins away, lest you hang on to them
in that way. Throw it all away!

Yet even "good Christians" hang on to the guilt of their
sins, be they real or imagined. A poll taken at a convention
of church women turned up the disturbing fact that guilt
is the heaviest burden these women bear! They to whom
"the gracious forgiveness of all your sins" is proclaimed again
and again are still tasting the bitterness of their selves, the
selves God has forgiven but they themselves refuse to forgive!
They continue to despise themselves, hate themselves, and
to brood over past sins. Yet they would be shocked if someone were to say to their faces, "So! You love your sin more
than you love your Savior!" They would be hurt if they were
told that the direction of their distress was *away from God,*
that it amounted to defiance of God.

The fruits of this particular pukah are many. Rooted in
the sin of self-love, their names have the prefix *self:* self-
abasement, self-abhorrence, self-accusation, self-annulment,
self-conceit, self-congratulation (I am the *greatest* sinner),
self-contempt, self-defeat, self-depreciation, self-destruc-
tion, self-disparagement, self-hatred, self-loathing, self-
mortification, self-pity, self-pride, self-scorn, self-torment,
self-torture.

What a morbid crowd! Who would ever invite such a
brood of vipers into one's innermost being? Yet the person
who says, "I can accept God's forgiveness, but I cannot, I
will never, forgive myself," throws the door of the psyche

91

open to this sickly mob. Anyone who hosts such a pitiful pack must go through life dolefully singing, "do—do—do—do" on the spiritual musical scale and never even ascend to sol, to say nothing of "fa—la—la." Or "Alleluia!" Kierkegaard likened do—o—o—le—ful Christians who live in this state to people who erect beautiful houses looking out on splendid panoramas and live in the basements.

Those who are stopped at the border of the state of forgiveness by the pukah, "I can accept *God's* forgiveness, but I cannot and I will not ever forgive myself" need to take to heart John's words of reassurance: "By this we shall know that we are of the truth, and reassure our hearts before him whenever our hearts condemn us; for God is greater than our hearts" (1 John 3:19-20). *For God is greater than our hearts!* Therefore, stop looking at the submerged iceberg of your sin, stop weighing it, measuring it, studying it, and bemoaning it. Know that it was there, that the tip was not the whole of it—but know, also, *that it is forgiven.* God is greater than your heart! God's love is so infinite and so infinitely thermal that it melts the highest of icebergs. God's love is inconceivable. Believe it! Believe that God loves you more than you can conceive. God's forgiveness is incomprehensible. Believe it! God loves you in your sin and with your sin!

Pukah 4. There are some people I cannot forgive.

There are many versions of this same theme:

"I would like to forgive him, but I don't see how it would help."

"I'll forgive her if she asks for forgiveness, but she never will, so. . .!"

"I did so much for that person, and he has paid me with nothing but injury."

"Only God can forgive a person like that, and after all I'm not God!"

"Forgive my mother-in-law? That woman who is constantly reproaching me to my face, criticizing me behind my back, interfering in our family life, playing the martyr? You gotta be kidding!"

"Forgive my daughter-in-law, who has turned my son against me, keeps my grandchildren away from me, and ridicules me to them? Impossible!"

"Forgive my parents for making me a psychic cripple by loving me too little? That's asking a bit much!"

"Forgive our children for being so cold and indifferent to us in our old age after all we did for them when they were young? They don't deserve our forgiveness!"

"Forgive our children for disappointing our expectations for them? After all, think of all our self-sacrifices so that they could achieve the money, power, and success we denied ourselves—only to see them fail!"

It is tragically true that all of us are warped and wounded in some way by being loved too little or too unwisely. And we, in turn, warp and wound others by loving too little or too unwisely. We are all victims of slights and hurts, and we in turn victimize others by *our* slights and hurts. And we can never become free from these warps and wounds unless we recognize them and forgive them—or seek forgiveness for them. If sons can never forgive their mothers for smothering them in supermom love, they will forever seek vengeance on and make targets of all other women. They will cease to be victims only when they can and do forgive that woman in their lives who sacrificed them on the altar of her self-love, all the time believing that she was being supremely self-less.

True, we can never forgive sins as God forgives. But God *expects* us to do it. If it were not possible for us to do it, God would not expect it. God has placed within us the capacity to do what he expects. God not only expects it— God commands it.

> Even if you are angry you must not sin: never let the sun set on your anger, or else you will give a devil a foothold. . . . Be friends with one another, and kind, and forgiving each other as readily as God forgives you in Christ (Eph. 4:26, 32 JB).

> Bear with one another; forgive each other as soon as a quarrel begins. The Lord has forgiven you; now you must do the same (Col. 3:13 JB).

As for what Christ thinks of our excuses for being unable to forgive some people, read again his description of the new spirit in the kingdom of God. What is the Sermon on the Mount but a sketch of the state of forgiveness! Here forgiveness is not something you and I give, grant, or bestow. It is a spirit, the spirit of reconciliation. It is love. As Kierkegaard said in *Works of Love:* "Long, long before the enemy thinks of seeking reconciliation, the lover is already reconciled with him." Consider the prodigal's father eagerly watching down the road, watching and waiting for his son's return. His heart was already reconciled with him and was leaning toward him. The prodigal's father lived in the state of forgiveness.

But in the terrible freedom God granted his earth children, the choice to seek and receive forgiveness from God and from others (or to forgive ourselves and to forgive others)—is ours. In a way we write our own ending to the "Whodunnit?" detective story of our lives. Like the Choose Your Own Adventure stories for children, we can choose from many possible endings. Whether we end up living in the state of forgiveness or are stopped at the border by this pukah is a matter of choice.

Pukah 5. There are some people from whom I cannot receive forgiveness.

"Offenders never pardon," says an old proverb.

Somewhere in one of his splendid books Charles Williams wrote, "Many promising reconciliations have broken down because while both parties are prepared to forgive, neither party came prepared to be forgiven." Our humanness says, "Forgive my enemies—yes, but spare me their miserable, wretched forgiveness!"

When one does not live in the state of forgiveness but considers forgiveness to be something one gives and bestows or receives and accepts, then the old natural law that it is harder to receive than to give is in force. Then it is very noble to give forgiveness but very humbling to have to receive it. Once again Kierkegaard's keen eye penetrated to the psychological depth of this pukah.

Why is it so difficult for the offending party to forgive or accept forgiveness? Because it is so difficult to humble oneself under one's own guilt. This accounts for the hate whereby the world never forgives its having wronged the good. . . . In order to be able to forgive completely, the guilty party must feel his guilt infinitely—otherwise he prefers to be angry at the one he has wronged, or at least to avoid him, to shun his forgiveness. To accept the forgiveness of one wronged is the humiliation he cannot bear—which is why the offending party never forgives.

There are hundreds of books about human sexuality, but few—pitifully few—of them speak of sin, guilt, despair, and forgiveness. Six months of marriage is sufficient to make anyone sober-minded about living together " 'til death do us part." After six months of marriage many a marriage partner is assailed with the feeling of "wanting out." Many do in fact finalize and legalize their disillusionment and alienation in divorce. Alienation and not forgiveness has been domesticated and normalized and made the modern way of life. Forgiving and seeking forgiveness from the marriage partner for failing to live up to each other's romantic expectations seems to have become ridiculous. But how much more ridiculous it is that marriage partners forget that the magnitude of God's forgiveness of them in Christ makes it ridiculous for them not to forgive each other!

Long ago George Herbert wrote a poem he called "Giddinesse."

> Surely if each one saw another's heart,
> There would be no commerce,
> No sale or bargaine pass; all
> would disperse
> and live apart.

True, too sadly true! But not if two hearts—the one that sees and the one that is seen—are in the state of forgiveness, in the wholesome relationship that forgives in advance and cannot be taken by surprise, for it is armed against any disappointment or frustration by the forgiveness it has received from God through Christ Jesus.

Pukah 6. So I am forgiven, but what about my relapses into sin? Does not the doctrine of the forgiveness of sins make it possible for me to sin my way merrily to salvation?

The early Christians, most of whom of course were not born-and-brought-up Christians but were adult converts to Christianity, preferred late Baptism. Believing that penance, like Baptism, was unrepeatable, some postponed Baptism until the very end of their lives. Constantine (272-377), the first Christian emperor of Rome, was not baptized until the end of his life. Thus he became the only unbaptized president of an ecumenical council, the Council of Nicaea, which gave its name to the Nicene Creed in A.D. 325. In 373, Ambrose, the popular governor of Milan, was persuaded against his will to become bishop, which meant that he had to be baptized, confirmed, ordained as a priest, and consecrated as a bishop all within a week! It was the powerful preaching of Bishop Ambrose that was instrumental in converting Augustine to the Christian faith. And it was Augustine who reminded Christians that God is not a one-time-only forgiver but a God who forgives again and again and again.

Although it is true that our sins are forgiven through Christ, we are not snatched as if by magic out of our old condition. Indeed, when we have seen the light of Christ we see our sins ever more clearly. Who can see dirt in the dark? The increased knowledge of God's will that we have in Christ increases our consciousness of sin. But the consciousness of the forgiveness of our sins buoys us up, keeps us from despair, and gives us the crazy courage to live confidently and joyfully.

It was also Augustine who said, "Certainly God has promised you forgiveness, but he has not promised you tomorrow." In other words, the guilt is forgiven, but the consequences of our sins remain. And the probability that we will sin again. So what is new, then? The reassuring consciousness that my guilt was forgiven, is forgiven, and will be forgiven. Thus one can cheerfully say: "I have been imperfect, I am still imperfect, I will go on being imperfect. I have fallen, I do fall, I will fall again—but in Christ Jesus I have a new relationship to God. I will never fall out of relationship to God—no more than a child falls out of relationship to loving parents by a naughty act."

"It seems to you that God can no longer forgive you because you have sinned once again," wrote Kierkegaard, "that Christ can no longer pray for you—O think again! He allowed himself to be born, He endured thirty-four years of poverty and wretchedness, was persecuted, mocked, and finally crucified—in order to save you, too—and then He would not want to forgive you if you turn repentantly to Him!"

As for "sinning my way merrily to salvation"—how silly! Just as a child who is forgiven a serious wrongdoing by loving parents would not perversely do the same thing again but in gratitude will seek to please the parents, so I in gratitude to God for the forgiveness of my sins will strive to sin no more. But I soon discover that I cannot do it on my own strength. My human striving needs the divine encouragement, support, and power of the Holy Spirit, whose specific task is to work for my sanctification. My relationship to God is intact, my forgiveness is complete, but my sanctification is not. So come, Holy Spirit!

10

Forgiveness Is a Work as Well as a Grace

Then Peter came up and said to him, "Lord, how often shall my brother sin against me, and I forgive him? As many as seven times?" Jesus said to him, "I do not say to you seven times, but seventy times seven."

"Therefore the kingdom of heaven may be compared to a king who wished to settle accounts with his servants. When he began the reckoning, one was brought to him who owed him ten thousand talents; and as he could not pay, his lord ordered him to be sold, with his wife and children and all that he had, and payment to be made. So the servant fell on his knees, imploring him, 'Lord, have patience with me, and I will pay you everything.' And out of pity for him the lord of that servant released him and forgave him the debt. But that same servant, as he went out, came upon one of his fellow servants who owed him a hundred denarii; and seizing him by the throat he said, 'Pay what you owe.' So his fellow servant fell down and besought him, 'Have patience with me, and I will pay you.'

He refused and went and put him in prison till he should pay the debt. When his fellow servants saw what had taken place, they were greatly distressed, and they went and reported to their lord all that had taken place. Then his lord summoned him and said to him, 'You wicked servant! I forgave you all that debt because you besought me; and should not you have had mercy on your fellow servant, as I had mercy on you?' And in anger his lord delivered him to the jailers, till he should pay all his debt. So also my heavenly Father will do to every one of you, if you do not forgive your brother from your heart."

Matthew 18:21-35

Indeed, if someone refused to understand that forgiveness, too, is a burden to be borne, even though a light burden, he is taking forgiveness in vain. Forgiveness is not to be earned—that heavy it is not; but neither is it to be taken in vain—it is not that light either. Forgiveness is not to be paid for, that costly it is not—it cannot be paid for; but neither is it to be accepted as nothing, for that it is too dearly bought.

Søren Kierkegaard

The perfect Christian state is that in which our duty and our pleasure are the same, when what is right and true is natural to us, and in which God's service is perfect freedom.

Cardinal Newman

Prayer Meditation

We thank you for your forgiving love, our Father, but oh, Father, you are not yet done! There is so much more to forgive! Forgive us for making forgiveness only a private matter between you and our individual selves, for making it a "God-and-me" affair. Forgive us for accepting only one

102

part of grace—forgiveness and reconciliation. Forgive us for so seldom considering our need to forgive others and to be forgiven by them as well as by you. Forgive us for not seeing that justification by faith also means our opportunity and responsibility to correct injustices. Forgive us for not seeing that reunion with you through your Son means our reunion with others from whom we are alienated. Our Father, this work is too big for us! Send us your Holy Spirit! Amen.

Someone analyzed the mental age of the audiences Jesus addressed and determined that they averaged out to about 12 years. Sensitive to his audience, Jesus spoke in the simple language that they could understand. How could he have expressed more simply: "Blessed are the peacemakers, for they shall be called the sons of God." "If you are offering your gift at the altar, and there remember that your brother has something against you, leave your gift there before the altar and go; first be reconciled to your brother, and then come and offer your gift." "If anyone strikes you on the right cheek, turn to him the other also." "Love your enemies and pray for those who persecute you." "For if you forgive men their trespasses, your heavenly Father also will forgive you; but if you do not forgive men their trespasses, neither will your Father forgive your trespasses."

No one needs to run for a dictionary or a Bible commentary to understand Christ's words about forgiveness. Does that make forgiving or being forgiven as easy as saying "Excuse me" when you bump into someone or "I'm sorry!"

if you step on someone's toe? Is it as simple as apologizing to Uncle Don for calling him a big bore when you really do think he is a big bore, but you didn't want him to overhear you say it? Is it as simple as indulgently overlooking a slight or as being magnanimous about losing a chairmanship to someone who can never do as good a job as you could have done had you won? Is it as meaningless as saying, "Forget it!" to the paperboy who delivered the Sunday paper long past breakfast, when you are in the habit of reading it while you drink your coffee? Is it as pleasurable as generously tipping the waitress who brought you lukewarm roast lamb on a cold plate? Or indulgently giving up your favorite TV programs so that the teenagers can watch the basketball tournament?

None of these occasions merits forgiveness. They ask only for ordinary human decency—for tolerance, kindness, a sense of humor. Forgiveness is not something lightly earned by lightly apologizing or saying, "I'm sorry!" Nor is it a favor bestowed by saying, "Forget it!" or "That's OK!" It is not tenderness toward bores, tolerance toward people who rub you the wrong way, permissiveness toward the impertinent. It is not banishing standards, values, judgment, rules, discipline—or watering them down to vapidity. Forgiveness is not social etiquette. It is not forgetting, excusing, condoning, overlooking, and smoothing over. Even a currently popular word, *acceptance,* becomes cheap and weak and soft beside forgiveness, which has nothing cheap or weak or soft about it. Christ did not come to this earth to share our broken human lives as the incarnate niceness of a God for whom it was as nice and natural to forgive as it is nasty and natural for his earth children to hurt and wound and

104

sever their relationship to him and to each other. "How natural of God to forgive! How nice of Christ to die on the cross!"

"No!" shouts that tough theologian, P. T. Forsythe. "If there be one thing in the world for ever supernatural, it is real forgiveness—especially on the scale of redemption. It is natural only to the supernatural. The natural man does not forgive. He resents and revenges. His wrath smolders till it flashes. And the man who forgives easily, jauntily, and thoughtlessly when it is a real offense is neither natural nor supernatural but subnatural. He is not only less than God, he is less than man."

No, forgiveness is not easy, and the state of forgiveness is not a perfect Christian state where human beings are tuned in to an easy and comfortable forgiveness, a static-free FM, "forgiveness modulation." No discordant criticizing, ridiculing, scolding, nagging, reproaching. No divorces, no litigation, no factions, no church denominations, no political parties. Every citizen is born again with a brand-new nature that does not judge others, finds no fault in others, is never envious, resentful.

Ah, no! Even Christ's hand-picked apostles feuded!

And after some days Paul said to Barnabas, "Come, let us return and visit the brethren in every city where we proclaimed the word of the Lord, and see how they are." And Barnabas wanted to take with them John called Mark. But Paul thought best not to take with them one who had withdrawn from them in Pamphylia, and had not gone with them to the work. And there arose a sharp contention, so that they separated from each other; Barnabas took Mark with him and sailed away to Cyprus, but Paul chose Silas and departed, being commended by the brethren to the grace of the Lord (Acts 15:36-40).

Forgiveness is a work as well as a grace, and even the great preachers and proclaimers of God's love and grace and forgiveness had to and still have to work at making God's love and grace and forgiveness valid in their lives.

Father Zossima says in *The Brothers Karamazov:*

> I am sorry I can say nothing more consoling to you, for love in action is a hard and dreadful thing compared with love in dreams. Love in dreams is greedy for immediate action, rapidly performed and in the sight of all. Men will even give their lives if only the ordeal does not last long but is soon over, with all looking on and applauding as though on the stage. But active love is labor and fortitude.

Read these lines again, and read *forgiveness* where the word is *love.*

Real forgiveness is work and fortitude! " 'Tis not the dying for a faith that's so hard, Master Harry," William Thackeray has one of his characters say in his novel *Esmond.* "Every man of every nation has done that. 'Tis the living up to it that is difficult."

Late convert though he was, Augustine became one of the greatest theologians and preachers of the church. Once when his audience became audibly excited and stirred by his preaching, he stopped speaking, waited for silence, and then said quietly: "The words please you. I ask for good works!"

Luther, whose battle was against work righteousness, nevertheless saw the close connection between forgiveness

106

and good works and that the work of forgiveness and reconciliation confirmed and made manifest that we have received the forgiveness of sin. Forgiveness, he said, takes place in two ways: inwardly in the heart and outwardly in the works of forgiveness. Of all people, Luther would be the last to say that the working of forgiveness in either place—in the heart or out in the world—is easy. Characteristically, he used strong and dramatic words for it— "pulling Christ into the flesh"—and went on to say that "Christ can never be pulled into the flesh deeply enough."

Real forgiveness means a radical change in the heart. It means becoming a different person, a new person. And, says Frederick Buechner, "The process of being changed from a slob into a human being is no Sunday school picnic. Childbirth may on occasion be painless, but rebirth never."

In Shakespeare's *Hamlet*, Claudius, who had killed his brother, Hamlet's father, and taken both the dead king's throne and his wife, dramatically expresses the pain and difficulty of both the inward and outward work of forgiveness. He struggled with the desire to repent but found himself unwilling to restore the possessions his sin brought him, the profit gained by the murder of his brother.

O, my offence is rank, it smells to heaven;
It hath the primal eldest curse upon't,
A brother's murther! Pray can I not,
Though inclination be as sharp as will.
My stronger guilt defeats my strong intent,
And, like a man to double business bound,
I stand in pause where I shall first begin,
And both neglect. What if this cursed hand

Were thicker than itself with brother's blood,
Is there not rain enough in the sweet heavens
To wash it white as snow? Whereto serves mercy
But to confront the visage of offence?
And what's in prayer but this twofold force,
To be forestalled ere we come to fall,
Or pardon'd being down? Then I'll look up;
My fault is past. But, O, what form of prayer
Can serve my turn? 'Forgive me my foul murther'?
That cannot be; since I am still possess'd.
Of those effects for which I did the murther—
My crown, mine own ambition, and my queen.
May one be pardon'd and retain th' offence?
In the corrupted currents of this world
Offence's gilded hand may shove by justice,
And oft 'tis seen the wicked prize itself
Buys out the law; but 'tis not so above.
There is no shuffling; there the action lies
In his true nature, and we ourselves compell'd,
Even to the teeth and forehead of our faults,
To give in evidence. What then? What rests?
Try what repentance can. What can it not?
Yet what can it when one cannot repent?
O wretched state! O bosom black as death!
O limed soul, that, struggling to be free,
Are more engag'd! Help, angels! Make assay.
Bow, stubborn knees; and heart with strings of
steel,
Be soft as sinews of the new-born babe!
All may be well.

(Claudius kneels.)

While Claudius was praying, Hamlet stole up behind
him, sword in hand, and resolved to kill him and avenge
his father's death. However, he could not do so while

Claudius was praying, lest he send his soul to heaven! He resolved to put up his sword until he found Claudius "drunk asleep; or in his rage; or in the incestuous pleasure of his bed; at gaming, swearing, or about some act that has no relish of salvation in it." Meanwhile Claudius could not truly repent because he could not follow through and make restitution for his wrongs. He rose from his knees.

> My words fly up, my thoughts remain below,
> Words without thoughts never to heaven go.

So one more unfulfilled occasion for true repentance and forgiveness went on the garbage heap! "But *Hamlet* is just a play. It's fictional!" someone says. So it is, but that does not diminish the Mount Everest of actual unfulfilled occasions. Unfulfilled occasions? A euphemism for outright rebellion and disobedience to the will of God! We do not lack in understanding Christ's words about forgiveness. We lack the will to obey them! Moreover, the refusal and rejection is not just discarded garbage. It is toxic material, PCBs that leak poison and cause cancer, whereas forgiving and being forgiven are positive acts of healing. The wound becomes strong and healthy flesh—and does not even leave a scar.

But the strongest and healthiest of human wills cannot cleanse the mind of hates and grudges and bitter memories. Even with the best of wills we cannot forgive ourselves for betraying the ideals of our youth. The soundest will is unable of itself to have an unquenchable spirit of love and forgiveness, cannot of itself achieve the victory of forgiving enemies. Transcendental meditation cannot do it. Eating natural foods cannot do it. Yogurt and yoga cannot do it.

Jogging and cross-country skiing cannot do it. Psychiatry can say, "Hang in there, baby!"—but does not speak of guilt, repentance, and forgiveness. Only the Holy Spirit can give me the willingness to be forgiving. I can never in all eternity forgive as God forgives, but the Holy Spirit can penetrate my weak will and make my impotent *I* a potent *we* that engages in the work of forgiveness and reconciliation in the world, starting in my own family and neighborhood and church.

The Holy Spirit infuses my poor, pinched, human willingness to forgive and makes it a divinely genuine willingness to which the one I weakly willed to forgive cannot say, "No, thanks!" Moreover, the Holy Spirit removes the impure motives that even my weak willingness to forgive can and does have.

Spirit power is the only power that makes the impossible possible! It is the only power that turns understanding into willing, into action. Will, says Emily Dickinson, is the manufacturing place.

> A Deed knocks first at Thought
> And then—it knocks at Will—
> That is the manufacturing spot
> and Will at Home and well
>
> It then goes out an Act
> Or is entombed so still
> That only to the ear of God
> Its Doom is audible—

To be forgiven and to know it is to change—by the help of the Spirit. To change is to exercise the law of forgiveness—by the help of the Spirit. To exercise the law of forgiveness is to act—by the help of the Spirit. Without the

110

Spirit, my human attempts flub and fizzle and fail—and are recorded in "The Book of the Non-Acts of You and the Non-Acts of Me."

To many people today the institutionalized church seems to be far removed from the Spirit-filled new believers who came together to share the Lord's Supper and express in words and songs and actions their thanksgiving to God for the love and forgiveness manifested to them in the death and resurrection of his Son. Yet a Swedish theologian, Einar Billing, said of this institutionalized church: "The Church is the forgiveness of sins to the people of Sweden." We likewise can say, "The church is the forgiveness of sins to the people of the United States of America, of Canada, Mexico...." Ah, centuries before that first Pentecost, the church was the forgiveness of sins to the people of God! Solomon said it again and again in his powerful prayer at the dedication of the temple in Jerusalem.

> "O Lord, God of Israel, there is no God like thee, in heaven above or on earth beneath, keeping covenant and showing steadfast love to thy servants who walk before thee with all their heart. . . . But will God indeed dwell on the earth? Behold, heaven and the highest heaven cannot contain thee; how much less this house which I have built! Yet have regard to the prayer of thy servant and to his supplication. . . .and of thy people Israel, when they pray toward this place; yea, hear thou in heaven thy dwelling place; and when thou hearest, forgive. . . . When thy people Israel are defeated before the enemy because they have sinned against thee, if they turn again to thee, and acknowledge thy name, and pray and make supplication to thee in this house; then hear thou in heaven, and *forgive* the sin of thy people Israel (1 Kings 8:23-33; italics added).

111

Do I hear someone say, "A magnificent prayer, but don't forget that the one who prayed that magnificent prayer built that magnificent temple with forced labor and bleeding taxes."

So he did, and I know a pillar of the church so full of resentment of his own children that he drove them out of his home and out of the church. And I know a faithful church member and church worker who is such a compulsive nagger that her husband stays at the office until he is sure that she has gone to bed. And I know myself. I know that I have a closet full of clothes and a Christ who says that if I have two coats I should give one away. I have cupboards full of food and a Christ who says, "Feed the hungry."

The spleeny pillar and the pious nagger and I belong to the church for the same reason Solomon built a church, because we are sinners and need the church. There and nowhere else we hear the Word that speaks to our condition and convicts us of our sin. There and nowhere else we hear God's will for us that tussles with our own selfish, self-centered wills. There and nowhere else we meet the forgiving Christ in the Lord's Supper. There more than anywhere else is our greatest hope for the change of heart that we know we need but are snail-slow about changing.

Come to think of it, the church is the only institution I know that provides the means of grace and forgives us for misusing it! Forgives us for not turning in God's pardoning love and going home from church to *be* pardoning love. Forgives us for understanding Christ's forgiveness as a means of grace that wipes the slate clean but not receiving forgiveness as a means of grace that makes *us* forgive. Forgives us for not making forgiveness a work as well as a grace. Amazing grace, that waits for sinners like Solomon, the spleeny pillar, the pious nagger, and me to love and forgive one another as God's grace has forgiven us!

11

And It Works!

I give you a new commandment:
love one another;
just as I have loved you,
you must also love one another.
By this love you have for one another,
everyone will know that you are my disciples.

John 13:33-35 JB

Little by little, the forgiven man starts to become a forgiving
man, the healed man to become a healing man, the loved
man to become a loving man. Sanctification is the second
stage in the process of salvation.

Frederick Buechner, Wishful Thinking

Prayer Meditation
Our Father, lead us into the pleasure of doing your will.
Amen.

Do I hear someone muttering: "You have preached and
pontificated about forgiveness, quoted gobs of Bible verses,

and told some beautiful stories. But *Les Miserables, Crime and Punishment, The Brothers Karamazov, Cry, the Beloved Country*—all those stories are fictional! Anyone can spin a yarn about the fictitious miraculous results of a fictitious act of forgiveness. Things like that do not happen in real life. In real life, people get murdered in their beds by escaped convicts and foolish women who give a tramp a bite to eat get raped and robbed, and a kind old gentleman who picks up a hitchhiker is killed and dumped in the ditch."

So you want real-life stories? OK! How about one out of my own childhood that I told in *From This Good Ground*. I tell it especially for those who may think that children take guilt and alienation lightly, do not understand the despair of guilt and alienation, and therefore cannot understand the dimensions of forgiveness. The "threesome" in the story are myself, age nine; my sister Eleanor, age six; and my brother, age four. The time is the early 1920s, the month of June. The scene is our north-central Wisconsin farm.

One of our self-created pastimes during the making of the hay ended in tragedy and points up the responsibility thrust upon me as the oldest member of the threesome. Maude, an old and retired horse, was left at the barn to pull the hayfork with its clutch of hay up to a pulley track where it slid back into the dark cavern of the hayloft and was dumped into the haymow. All the skittishness had drained out of faithful old Maude and she was judged safe enough for us kids to lead and to ride up and down the slope to the haybarn. We were not warned against the horse but against following behind the whiffletree lest something break and the whiffletree be catapulted back and kill us. There was always a true-life story to back up these admonitions.

But no one thought to warn us of what eventually happened, for our own capricious imaginations were not to be anticipated. While father and the boys were in the field, we three decided to lead Maude, hitched to the hayfork rope, up and down the slope. We took turns leading the horse, the other two standing at the top of the slope behind the pulley through which the rope snaked. While I was leading Maude, Bernard, suddenly dissatisfied with the limp and laggard way the rope was rising to the pulley, grabbed the rope and braced his four-year-old body against the pull. A knot slithered up and pulled his left and foremost hand into the pulley. Maude and I heard his scream and stopped. I turned and saw the frayed and mangled flesh that never again shaped a tolerable hand.

Our treble screams brought father and the boys across the field with the hay wagon lurching and the work horses at full gallop. It brought mother running from the kitchen, her face contorted with fear. But it was another contortion that sent me to hide in the farthest and darkest corner of the empty sheepshed.

"Now see what you have done!" she cried, her face dark with anger, as she and father drove off to the hospital twelve miles away with Bernard still screaming between them, his mutilated hand swathed in clean boiled towels.

I did not question the accusation. I did not dodge the guilt. After all, mother was right. I was the oldest. I should have known better. Lying face down on the musty straw of the sheepshed, I cried and keened and assumed the whole load of guilt. Desperate suicidal plans marched through my mind, but fortunately I eventually fell asleep and could not attempt them. In a stupor of despair I slept hours, and it was hours before they found me. Fortunately, too, it was mother, my chief accuser, who found me, and her relief when the inert form of her sixth child stirred under her groping, searching hand was such that she burst into tears.

"Stakkars! Stakkars! You couldn't help it! I didn't mean what I said!"

And I awoke to weep afresh, but this time mother's tears mingled with mine, and the miraculous power of forgiving love began its healing. I was accepted back into the family, and no one ever blamed me again for the deformed hand. Not even Bernard. By the grace of forgiveness, the adhesive that held our decemvirate and triumvirate together did not yield, proving again that love is tougher than iron, stronger than steel.

My next real-life story illustrating that forgiveness works is from Philip Hallie's book *Lest Innocent Blood Be Shed*, the story of a French village which in World War II concealed Jews from the Nazis and helped them to escape being sent to death camps. Eventually Pastor Trocme, the inspiration for and leader of the underground movement, was arrested. While her husband was being allowed to gather together a few essentials for his imprisonment, Magda Trocme invited the men who arrested her husband to dinner. Later her friends and neighbors vented their indignation upon her. How could she be so forgiving and so decent to *those* men? Thereupon Magda Trocme herself became indignant. What did they mean? It was dinner time. Dinner was ready. The men were standing there. What did her friends and neighbors mean by such foolish words as "forgiving" or "decent"? What did that have to do with goodness?

The other incident is in Corrie ten Boom's book *The Hiding Place*. She told of being in a church in Munich after World War II and recognizing a former S.S. man who had been one of the guards in the processing center at Ravensbruck. She and her sister and the other women prisoners had had to disrobe before the eyes of the guards and listen to their mocking jeers. The former S.S. man came up after the meeting, where she had spoken about the forgiveness of sins in Christ Jesus. He expressed his gratitude for her message. "To think that, as you say, He has washed my sins away." Corrie ten Boom related that she looked at his hand thrust out to shake hers and was filled with anger and vengeful thoughts. But Jesus Christ had died for this man. Was she going to ask for more? Desperately she prayed for the power to forgive him: "Jesus, I cannot forgive him. Give me your forgiveness."

"As I took his hand the most incredible thing happened," Corrie ten Boom wrote. "From my shoulder along my arm and through my hand a current seemed to pass from me to him, while into my heart sprang a love for this stranger that almost overwhelmed me. And so I discovered that it is not on our forgiveness any more than on our goodness that the world's healing hinges, but on his. When he tells us to love our enemies, he gives, along with the command, the love itself."

"Self-yeast of spirit a dull dough sours," wrote Gerard Manley Hopkins. Not only that, self-yeast cannot raise the dull dough to forgiveness. It takes forgiveness yeast and Spirit yeast to do that. Christians who have received this double-action yeast are no longer weak, soft, and wavering. Forgiven, they forgive, relying on the promise of the power of the Holy Spirit. They become God's coworkers in the work of handing on the reconciliation they have received through God's Son. To their amazement they discover, as did Christ's coworkers, the apostles, that forgiveness really does work. It truly does heal old wounds and leave no scars.

It does in truth unclench clenched fists. It does indeed help parents forgive their children and children forgive their parents. It really does get neighbors who have not spoken for years to speak to each other.

It worked for the apostle Paul and helped him forgive John Mark for becoming homesick on the first missionary journey and returning to Jerusalem. Paul's "sharp contention" with Barnabas overtaking John Mark on the next journey shows that even Christ's handpicked apostles feuded. (What strange comfort we find in such evidence! Somehow it is comforting to know that there are earthquakes in other human relationships, cracks on the surface of other families' lives, as well as leaks in their houses and mites and mealy bugs on their houseplants!) But that feud between Paul and Barnabas and John Mark was healed. There is no account of it in the New Testament, but there *is* the proof of the healing, proof that the parties concerned worked at forgiveness—and it worked! While under arrest in Rome, Paul wrote a letter to the Christians in Colossae in which he said:

Aristarchus my fellow prisoner greets you, and Mark the cousin of Barnabas (concerning whom you have received instructions—if he comes to you, receive him), and Jesus who is called Justus. These are the only men of the circumcision among my fellow workers for the kingdom of God, and they have been a comfort to me (Col. 4:10-12).

In what was perhaps Paul's last letter, his "will and testament," written shortly before his martyrdom in 67, Paul wrote to his beloved fellow-worker, Timothy:

Do your best to come to me soon. For Demas, in love with this present world, has deserted me and gone to

120

Thessalonica; Crescens has gone to Galatia, Titus to Dalmatia. Luke alone is with me. Get Mark and bring him with you; for he is very useful in serving me (2 Tim. 4:9-11).

Paul did not make a "big deal" of the reconciliation with Barnabas and John Mark. Nor is reconciliation a big deal if one lives in the state of forgiveness. At least it was not so for J. W. Stevenson, a pastor in a small Scottish village, his first parish. In *God in My Unbelief* he wrote of the festering alienations he discovered in his parish. He discovered that he did not believe that anything would or could change—and that his parishioners did not want anything to change. Eventually the truth pierced through to him that his unbelief was in fact atheism, a disbelief in the gospel of forgiveness and its power to reconcile and to heal. He began in earnest to serve as a minister of reconciliation in his parish. *It worked!*

Among the people the gentle pastor persuaded to forgive each other were two elderly women living next door to each other. Friends and neighbors for years, they had "fallen out" over something so minor and silly that if it was mentioned at all in the book I cannot remember it. The pastor visited each of the two women, speaking the gospel Word of forgiveness, and it pricked their hearts. But how to humble themselves to ask each other's forgiveness, when words that were not related to the births, deaths, and marriages in the village were so hard to come by? One of the women was nearsighted and for years had been unable to thread a needle. Until the rupture in the relationship, she had always taken the needle to be threaded by her neighbor. Shortly after the pastor had visited the two fallen-out friends, the nearsighted

121

neighbor opened her gate to go to the green grocer, and with her good distance vision saw a threaded needle sticking in her gatepost. Reconciliation does not always require words! A look, a hug, a freshly baked loaf of bread, an apple pie—there are countless eloquent ways to say "Forgive me!" or "I forgive you!"

Another true-life story that illustrates that forgiveness is a work and that it works is that of a bishop who in every way matches the good bishop in *Les Miserables*. It is also the story of a father who in every way matches the father in Christ's parable of the prodigal son, the father who is a model for the state of forgiveness. I shall tell the story and make no comment on it, for any comment would be a sacrilege!

When Muslim fanatics attempted to kill the bishop of the Christian Church in Iran, he fled to the island of Cyprus. On May 6, 1980, the Muslims succeeded in murdering the bishop's son, Bahram. Upon receiving news of his son's death, the bishop wrote a prayer. Danish missionaries translated it into Danish, and it was published in a church bulletin in a Danish church, where my husband and I saw it. We translated it from Danish to English and give it to you in a version twice-removed from the language in which it was written.

> O God, we are not thinking only of Bahram, but also of his murderers.
> Not because they killed him in the springtime of his youth and made our hearts bleed and our tears to flow.
> Not because this crime has cast shame upon our land among the nations of the world.
> But because through this crime, by this sacrifice, we can follow more closely in your footsteps.

The dreadful fire of grief burns up all selfishness, all selfish demands in us.

Its flame discloses the depths of baseness and mistrust, the dimension of hatred and sinfulness in human nature.

It shows us as never before our need to fasten our trust in God's love, in the death and resurrection of Christ.

God's love in the death and resurrection of Christ:
a love that releases us from hating our persecutors,
a love that gives us patience, forbearance, faithfulness, humility, generosity, and courage,
a love stronger than any mind, that fixes our certainty upon God's ultimate victory and his eternal plan with the church and with the world,
a love that will teach us to be ready for our own death.

God, Bahram's blood has nourished the fruit of the Spirit in our souls.

When his murderers stand before you on the day of judgment, remember the fruits of the Spirit with which you have enriched our lives.

From Gordon and Charlotte Rasmussen of St. Olaf College I recently received another prayer by a living saint. They had just returned from a visit to the Lutheran Theological College in Umpumulo, Natal, Republic of South Africa, where they had taped a service on Soweto Day, the day black Africans are forbidden to commemorate, but the day of anguish they will never forget. The prayer was prayed spontaneously and out of the heart of the black pastor who must remain unnamed. This prayer, too, is roughly translated from the original language.

Heavenly Father, teach us to understand our position and situation in this land where you have placed us. We

123

believe, Lord, that it was not a mistake that you created us and gave us this color. It sometimes follows us and brings persecution and suffering upon us. We know, O God, that you had a purpose when you created us, and we think that you have not abandoned us.

Sometimes it happens that we fail to see your purpose. Teach us, O Lord, to learn lessons from the events we experience in this country. Help us to glory that you are with us. Teach us to forgive where we have been hurt. Teach our young people to look to you.

We are thankful for the message that Jesus Christ came to this earth to set the oppressed free. O Lord, make this message a reality to us, especially to those who are beginning to lose hope. Your Word is always to be trusted. Lord, help us not to give up. Help us to see the promised land. Help us not to remember back where you want us to forget. Help us to look forward.

Give your Spirit to all who are here this day—not to demonstrate hate or defeat, but to glorify you in our suffering because we are convinced that Jesus Christ is for us. We think of those families who lost their loved ones on this day and are remembering them today. Comfort them and give them strength in the hope of the resurrection. You are the way and you are the life. That is the only life—a life where no race will be superior to another and all your children will be equal.

Lord, keep our country from experiencing again those happenings of 1976. Give us the best way to achieve our freedom. We are not here judging, for we know that in every way you are the Lord. You are the One, and we are just relating to you in these darkest times. We are thankful for the Word we have had this morning. Let it be the Word we think about all day today, your Word only, nothing else. Amen.

In his last book, *Lazarus,* the French author André Malraux roamed through the memories of his encounters with

124

death. One memory took him back to a Nazi extermination camp in the last days of World War II. Malraux was with the liberating troops that entered the camp, heaped with corpses, "their backs bristling with vertebrae." A journalist who was accompanying the liberators interviewed an emaciated prisoner who had only enough breath of life left within him to say: "You see, there's no room left in our hearts except for forgiveness."

Before such living witnesses to the power of forgiveness, we can only ask: How can it be that those who have the *most* to forgive *have the most forgiveness in their hearts*—and we who have so little to forgive even find it hard to pray for those against whom we have only a mean and petty grudge? Does the work of forgiveness become something else—for the person who works at it?